Random Acts of Kindness

ALSO AVAILABLE FROM CONARI PRESS

*More Random Acts of Kindness*
*Kids' Random Acts of Kindness*
*The Practice of Kindness*
*The Community of Kindness*
*Practice Random Acts of Kindness*

# RANDOM
## ACTS
### OF
# KINDNESS

THE EDITORS OF CONARI PRESS

**Foreword by Daphne Rose Kingma**
**Introduction by Dawna Markova, Ph.D.**

Conari Press

Cover Illustration: Gary R. Phillips
Hand-lettering: Lilly Lee
Cover Design: Claudia Smelser/Maxine Ressler
Book Design: Maxine Ressler

ISBN-10: 1-57324-853-3
ISBN-13: 978-1-57324-853-2

*This has been previously cataloged by the Library of Congress*

Random acts of kindness / by the editors of Conari Press

    p.   cm.
   ISBN: 0-943233-43-7

   1. Kindness--Quotations, maxims, etc.   I. Conari Press.
BJ1533.K5R36  1993                       92-38017
177'.7--dc20                              CIP

Printed in the United States of America

DATA  10  9  8  7  6  5

For Anne Herbert,
the woman who started the movement

# The Power of Kindness

It is a tragedy that in 2002 the mention of tragedy has itself become commonplace. So much has been said, so many flags waved since the heart of America was opened on September 11, 2001, that it seems almost opportunistic to mention it yet again.

And yet the events of that day are the new backdrop against which all our deeds, beautiful and kind, heinous or destructive, will now be silhouetted.

In such a world kindness is not a frill; it is a spiritual necessity. Indeed, where we once might have thought of random acts of kindness as charming, delightful, or even amusing, we cannot but see them now as the moment-by-moment, day-by-day acts of love that pierce the night sky with millions of pinpoints of light, the deed-by-deed creation of a world of hopeful possibilities—indeed, of love.

For what we now know in the cells of ours souls—what we have always known, but often forget—is that every corner of our universe—and of our ourselves—is claimed by either goodness or ungoodness, by that which springs from love and gathers us all closer into the basket of life, or that which rises from unlove and makes our journey an arduous ordeal; and that for love to prevail we must practice it by teaspoonfuls, and bucketfuls and floods, in nanoseconds and minutes, week after week, for our entire lives.

The practice of kindness is the daily, friendly, homely caring form of love. It is both humble—a schoolboy bringing his teacher a bouquet of dandelions—and exalted—a fireman giving his life to save someone else's. Kindness is love with hands and hearts and minds. It is both whimsical—causing our faces to crack into a smile—and deeply touching—causing our eyes to shimmer with tears. And its miraculous nature is such that the more acts of kindness we offer, the more of them we have to give, for acts of kindness are always drawn from the endless well of love.

Kindness is twice blessed. It blesses the one who gives it with a sense of his or her own capacity to love, and the person who receives it with a sense of the beneficence of the universe. Kindness heals us, because it reminds us of our oneness, allows us to see ourselves in one another's eyes, to remember that eyes themselves are a miracle, that seeing is a gift, and that the other, no matter who he or she may be, is, in one way or another, a perfect reflection of ourselves.

The power of kindness is immense. It is nothing less, really, than the power to change the world.

Daphne Rose Kingma

.......................

Fear grows out of the things we think; it lives in our minds. Compassion grows out of the things we are, and lives in our hearts.

—*Barbara Garrison*

# Living from the Heart

I don't care what anyone else says. These are awful times. There is tension in people's faces. Children wear bruises and forget to laugh. People sleep under black plastic garbage bags and carry their worlds in shopping carts. Everyone shrugs and calls it compassion fatigue. Anxiety and despair swirl around in our minds like discarded newspapers with headlines that tell us to remain on continual alert, indefinitely.

Our souls are leaking. We are in a recession, and we are receding. We are not moving toward anything. We are receding away. Away from what terrifies us. Away from not enough. Away from chaos. Away from poverty. Away from random acts of violence, from hurricanes and drive-by shootings and child abuse and homelessness and AIDS and drug wars. We are both clutching each other and moving away at the same time. This little book you hold is more needed than ever.

When I was quite small my immigrant Russian grandmother told me that people in this country give from the wrong place. "When you give from here," she declared, pointing to her solar plexus, "it's like keeping a ledger book. That's not giving, that's trading. I give you three so you give me three. I sweep the floor so you carry the bundles."

She pushed the wisps of white hair out of her eyes with the back of her red hands, shaking her head back and forth, tsk-ing her tongue against her teeth. "You give your soul away when you give like that. Giving is supposed to be from here," she said, pointing to the center of her chest with a feathery finger. "When you give from your heart, it's not so you get anything back. There is no owing or owed. You just give because you want to give. When you give like this, it fills you up. Your heart can never run out. The more you give from there, the fuller you will be."

Then she wiped her hands on the impeccably clean white apron and pulled me to her. "You remember this, *ketzaleh*. Remember to give from your heart. When you give like this, there are no strangers. And remember to notice when other people give to you like this. Be sure to thank them."

Decades later, when I was struggling with a life-threatening disease, I traveled to a conference in

Washington, D.C., in search of answers. One of the speakers was Maya Angelou, a superb poet and writer. She spoke of surviving a childhood full of terror and violence. Her handholds through the darkness were countless gifts of beauty offered to her by authors and artists who never even knew she existed. "Their work inspired me, shaped my thinking, exposed me to what could be possible, " she recalled. "And I have never forgotten to say thank you for those random acts of kindness."

Without knowing it, without ever hearing my name or seeing the red knit dress I wore that day, Maya Angelou's words left fingerprints on my heart as if it were warm wax. I drove north seeing the world through a different lens. Fate was just as unfair as it had been when I drove to the conference, but my perception had changed. I could not stop thinking of the incredible gifts that had been bestowed on me every day of my life: the music of Tchaikovsky that swirled me 'round and 'round my awkward twelve-year-old body until I was a sugarplum fairy, the songs of Johnny Mathis that taught me how to love, Mark Twain's writing that taught me how to be brave, Monet's water lilies that taught me how to see, Mrs. McLean's garden that taught me about beauty in the back streets of Brooklyn. Each exit I passed on the interstate seemed to open another doorway to an embarrassment of riches I had forgotten to notice. The drive down to that conference had been fueled by my desire to get: get healed, get love, get friends, get attention. My return trip was just that: a return to my grandmother's lessons on giving from the heart, a return to remembering that I was connected to the starlit sky, the fiery sun rising, the warm brown earth. If a garden could blossom every spring, so could I! As I returned home, my soul stopped leaking.

Much of my adult life as a psychotherapist and thinking partner has been spent helping people sort through vast amounts of pain and fear, seeking ways to evolve beyond the crippling events of their histories, searching for ways to crumble the barriers behind which we all sometimes withdraw in defense and isolation. After my Maya Angelou-induced epiphany, I began asking people in workshops I was facilitating to join me in telling stories and writing acknowledgments about the random acts of kindness in their lives. For twenty minutes or so, the madness and brittleness of the world melted as men and women scrawled names, symbols, moments across the blank pages. Often, as one person would tell a story, another would nod his or her head, remembering a piece of music, a camp counselor, a man in a gas station, and add it to the page.

I asked people to consider the other side, the random acts of kindness they had performed in their lives. The room would fill with silence as if it were holding its breath. One or two people would speak shyly, as if they were giving a report to the Girl Scout leader at the Merit Badge ceremony. I had to encourage and cajole until a woman would admit that once she tied a string to all the bushes on her block, with a pack of Life Savers at the very end, a reward for anyone who was intrepid enough to follow her clue.

I don't believe this paralysis is due to compassion fatigue or a lack of caring. I believe we are trained to notice only deficits, only where we are stuck, only how we are suffering. We are trained to believe that we don't matter and that we cannot make a difference.

But we can. The reaction of the people of New York City after September 11 proved that, like yeasted bread dough, under the right circumstances, generosity and the desire to connect with one another rises in us naturally.

If violence and aggression are part of our human nature, then the opposite must also be true. We just forget. We are reminded many times a day of the darkest shadows we can cast. We need also to be reminded of the brilliant light we are capable of igniting.

Giving in this way is as effective as an anti-depressant. It is a positive contagion to counterbalance the negative contagion all around us. It is salve for wild attacks of loneliness, fear, and despair. It reconfirms that each of us does belong, that we are all interconnected. It's a way of giving unabashedly from your heart without giving yourself away.

The popularity of this little book, and the worldwide movement that has grown from it, is an indicator of how much spontaneous and anonymous generosity can be a life-cherishing force. It proves that it is possible to surpass the suffering in the world by adding to the joy.

Once you begin to perform and acknowledge random acts of kindness, you can no longer believe that what you do does not matter. It is as if you are dancing along a beach, making footprints on the edge where the shore-line meets the sea. No one is applauding. No one even sees your splendid gyrations of joy. You know full well that the tide will come and wash away the marks your dance has left. Still, the dance lives on in your heart, as does the simple, clean delight of being alive. As you are about to leave, you turn to face the shoreline one last time, and you notice a small child, fitting his feet into your tracks, spinning, giggling. In that one moment, you know there is less suffering in the world. You know you do make a difference.

In a time when so many people feel powerless and unrecognized, when there are so many miserable things that happen to so many wonderful people, there are moments when you must stomp your feet in indignation and make room for the expression of your outrage. But you must also create space in your life for the expression of gratitude. What has sustained your soul? What has inspired you to hold on when all else was pulling you over a cliff? You are, we all are, the culmination of an infinite number of improbable gifts from myriad nameless sources.

A warning is in order here: Acknowledging the random acts of kindness in your life, be they in nature, works of art, moments of truth, rescue, or redemption, will bind you to them in a certain way. You will enter into an active relationship with them. Though they may not have been addressed directly to you, bringing them into your awareness can create a homeopathic response. The tough shell around your heart will begin to crack ever so slightly, and the circumference of who you are will swell full and ripe, aching to reach.

It is time for all of us to risk our significance. It is our hope as contributors to this book that you will become part of the lineage, that you will be inspired by what we have breathed into these pages, and most of all, that you will practice random acts of kindness, so that which came to you as seed will be passed on to the next as blossom, and that which came to you as blossom will go on as fruit.

Dawna Markova, Ph.D.
Park City, Utah

# Spare Change

Every day I walk down the mall to get a cup of cappuccino, and every day I get hit up for spare change. Every day. The panhandlers all have these wonderful stories but you never know what to believe. After a while it gets to be an irritation, and then I find myself getting upset that I'm so irritated over what is really just spare change. One day this person came up to me and said, "I just ran out of gas. My car is about six blocks away from here I have two kids in the car and I'm just trying to get back home."

I said to myself, "Here we go again," but for some reason I gave him $10. Then I went on and got my cappuccino. As I was walking back to my office, I again saw the man standing by his car, which had run out of gas right in front of my office. Seeing me, he came over and said, "Thank you, but I don't need the full ten," and handed me $2.

Now I find that being asked for money no longer bothers me and I give whatever I can every time I get the chance.

......................

The quality of mercy is not strained;
it dropeth as the gentle rain from heaven;
upon the place beneath; it is twice blessed;
it blesseth him that giveth and him that takes.

—*William Shakespeare*

2

......................

*Agape* is understanding, creative, redemptive goodwill
toward all men. *Agape* is an overflowing love, which
seeks nothing in return. Theologians would say that it is
the love of God operating in the human heart. When you
rise to love on this level, you love all men not because
you like them, not because their ways appeal to you,
but you love them because God loves them.

—*Martin Luther King, Jr.*

# The Magic Dragon

Several years ago, when I was living in Chicago, I read in the newspaper about a little boy who had leukemia. Every time he was feeling discouraged or particularly sick, a package would arrive for him containing some little toy or book to cheer him up with a note saying the present was from the Magic Dragon. No one knew who it was. Eventually the boy died and his parents thought the Magic Dragon finally would come forth and reveal him or herself. But that never happened. After hearing the story, I resolved to become a Magic Dragon whenever I could and have had many occasions.

. . . . . . . . . . . . . . . . . . . . .

If there is any kindness I can show, or any good thing I can do to any fellow being, let me do it now, and not deter or neglect it, as I shall not pass this way again.

—*William Penn*

# Profound Connection

When I was in college I attended a lecture one evening on hypnosis by a blind hypnotist. At the end of the session we did a prolonged relaxation exercise, and I walked out of the room with a completely different body than I had walked in with. It was a very powerful experience of actually feeling myself as a body for the first time in my life. As I was walking across a bridge on the way home from the lecture, a man jumped out of the bushes and tried to hit me. It was really strange—here was a random act of physical violence coupled with an incredibly powerful experience of kindness that had moved me into my body. The violence is now just a memory, but the hypnotic journey into my body forever changed how I feel.

........................

Complete possession is proved only by giving. All you are unable to give possesses you.

—*André Gide*

# Ah, Bambini!

My husband and I were traveling in Italy with two small babies and an au pair. We would trade sightseeing time with the au pair so we could all visit the requisite churches and museums. But on this day we took the babies along, since we only had one day to go to Assisi and all of us urgently wanted to see it. The morning was wonderful—feeling like happy pilgrims, we read each other stories of St. Francis while the babies cooed and gurgled as we drove up the winding streets.

But by the end of a very hot day traipsing uphill and downhill in the 90-degree Italian sun, the two kids were crying nonstop. One was throwing up; the other had diarrhea. We were all irritable and exhausted, and we had a three-hour trip ahead of us to get back to Florence, where we were staying. Somewhere on the plains of Perugia we stopped at a little trattoria to have dinner.

Embarrassed at our bedraggled state and our smelly, noisy children, we sheepishly tried to sneak into the dining room, hoping we could silence the children long enough to order before they threw us out. The proprietor took one look at us, muttered "You wait-a here," and went back to the kitchen. We thought perhaps we should leave right then, but before we could decide what to do, he reappeared with his wife and teenage daughter. Crossing the dining room beaming, the two women threw out their arms, cried, "Ah, bambini!" and took the children from our arms, motioning us to sit at a quiet corner table. For the duration of a long and hospitable dinner, they walked the babies back and forth in the back of the dining room, cooing, laughing, and singing them to sleep in gentle, musical, Italian. The proprietor even insisted we stay and have an extra glass of wine after the babies were asleep! Any parent who has reached the end of his or her rope with an infant will appreciate that God had indeed sent us angels that day.

......................
My religion is very simple. My religion is kindness.

—*The Dalai Lama*


......................
We do not remember days, we remember moments.

—*Casare Pavese*

# Practice
# Random Acts of Kindness!

❧ Go to your child's class and talk about random acts of kindness. Then have the kids put together a booklet of the things they have done and those that have happened to them. Have them go home and teach parents the idea and come back to school the next day with stories from their families.

❧ Spend half an hour in a hospital emergency room and do one random act of kindness that presents itself.

❧ Offer to help people who could use the assistance to cross streets—seniors, the blind, small children. . . .

❧ Plant a tree in your neighborhood.

❧ The next time someone speaks to you, listen deeply without expecting anything.

❧ FIND someone you've been close to and sit back to back with her. For a few minutes disclose the random acts of kindness she has done for you while she just listens. Then switch and listen to the wonderful things you have done.

❧ YES, it's a drag, but why not put your shopping cart back in its appointed place in the parking lot?

❧ WRITE a note to the boss of someone who has helped you, thanking him or her for having such a great employee.

# The Answering Machine

Who would ever think that a telephone answering machine could change your life? I had just broken up from a long and very painful relationship and found myself suddenly in a new city without friends, without anything to do or any desire to do anything. I was like a listless blob of expended energy. Every day I would come home from work and just stare at the walls, sometimes crying but mostly just sitting and wondering if this cloud would ever go away.

I had bought an answering machine—why, I don't know, since nobody ever called me. One night I came home and the red light was flashing. I couldn't believe it, a phone call. When I played it back, a wonderful male voice started to apologize he had called the wrong number, and I burst into tears. But then he kept talking. He said my voice on the message had sounded so sad and he just wanted to tell me that it was OK to be sad, that being able to feel that sadness was important. His message went on for almost twenty minutes, just talking about how important it was to be able to go through the pain instead of running away from it, and how even though it probably seemed impossible now, things would get better. He never even said his name, but that message was, in a very important way, the beginning of my life.

......................

Put your heart, mind, intellect, and soul even to your smallest acts. This is the secret of success.

—*Swami Sivanada*

......................

The purpose of life is a life of purpose.

—*Robert Byrne*

# Gift to a Stranger

One night, while my lover was inside our house dying, I was on the porch smoking a cigarette. We lived on a dead-end street in a residential neighborhood that had very little foot traffic. But that night a woman walked by. I looked at her; she looked at me. After she had almost passed the house, she stopped, turned back, and walked up to the porch. She told me that she had taken the bus from Fresno to find a job, that she had left her children with someone, and if she did not get back that night, she would lose her kids. I called Greyhound and found out that the last bus to Fresno had left. We went around about what she would do. In the end I gave her $60 and she walked away. I did not then, nor do I now, believe her story. But I felt it was somehow important that I was being asked to give a gift to a stranger when someone I loved was about to die.

.....................

Do every act of your life
as if it were your last.

—*Marcus Aurelius*

# The Forgiven Debt

I had a client who owed me a good deal of money. Eventually she stopped seeing me, but each month I would send her a bill and receive no response. Finally I wrote to her and said, "I don't know what difficulty has befallen you that you are unable to pay me, but whatever it is, I'm writing to tell you your debt is forgiven in full. My only request is that at some point in your life, when your circumstances have changed, you will pass this favor on to someone else."

.....................

I am of the opinion that my life belongs to the community, and as long as I live, it is my privilege to do for it whatever I can. I want to be thoroughly used up when I die, for the harder I work, the more I live. Life is no "brief candle" to me. It is a sort of splendid torch which I have got hold of for a moment, and I want to make it burn as brightly as possible before handing it on to future generations.

—*George Bernard Shaw*

# Traffic Kindness

I was driving home from work on a crowded city street—parked cars on either side, traffic going about 25 miles per hour. I noticed a group of prepubescent boys on bikes, bobbing and weaving through traffic, being quite reckless and taking silly chances. Suddenly I realized that one of the boys was holding on to the door handle of my car, pedaling like mad to keep up. I honked and pulled over, gesturing for him to talk to me. First he took off, but then he circled back, looking sheepish and expecting a lecture, no doubt. His friends gathered around to see what would happen.

I got out of my car slowly, thinking about what kind of life this child must have to be willing to take such chances and wondering what I could possibly say that could make a difference. The words just tumbled out of my mouth. "I don't know you," I said quietly, "but I want you to live to a ripe old age with all your arms and legs intact." The boy looked at me, smiled, said "Thanks," and rode off. I don't know if I made a difference, but I pray I did.

# A Bouquet of Flowers

When I graduated from college I took a job at an insurance company in this huge downtown office building. On my first day, I was escorted to this tiny cubicle surrounded by what seemed like thousands of other tiny cubicles, and put to work doing some meaningless thing. It was so terribly depressing I almost broke down crying. At lunch—after literally punching out on a time clock—all I could think about was how much I wanted to quit, but I couldn't because I desperately needed the money.

When I got back to my cubicle after lunch there was a beautiful bouquet of flowers sitting on my desk. For the whole first month I worked there flowers just kept arriving on my desk. I found out later that it had been a kind of spontaneous office project. A woman in the cubicle next to me brought in the first flowers to try to cheer me up, and then other people just began replenishing my vase. I ended up working there for two years, and many of my best, longest-lasting friendships grew out of that experience.

# A Gift of Fear

Two days before my fiftieth birthday I had a heart attack. It was a most surprising random act of kindness. I had lived the previous thirty years of my life as a powerful, successful, and amazingly productive man. I had also lived so cut off from my emotions that I couldn't even fathom what the whole fuss about feelings was all about. I had worn out the efforts of three good women, took pride in my unfeeling logic, denied that there was anything wrong or missing in my life, and was prepared to march stubbornly forward.

Until I was felled and terrified by my own heart. That experience unlocked a lifetime of buried emotions. So, without knowing it, when the doctors revived me, they delivered me to a life fuller and more beautiful than I had ever imagined.

......................

If you bring forth what is inside of you, what you bring forth will save you. If you don't bring forth what is inside of you, what you don't bring forth will destroy you.

—*Jesus*

# The Old Dog

I used to jog through the park every morning, and I always went by an old woman who sat on a bench with a small, very old, mangy dog. One day I noticed her dog wasn't with her. For some reason I stopped and asked her where he was. Suddenly, tears started running down the lines in her face and she told me he had died the night before. I sat and talked with her for over an hour. Every day after that we would greet each other as I came by; sometimes I would stop and talk with her for a while. She was very lonely but also very strong, and to this day I think of her when I'm sad, and it makes me smile.

......................

We cannot live only for ourselves. A thousand fibers connect us with our fellow men; and among those fibers, as sympathetic threads, our actions run as causes, and they come back to us as effects.

—*Herman Melville*

# PRACTICE
## RANDOM ACTS OF KINDNESS!

- ❧ BUY a roll of brightly colored stickers and stick them on kids' shirts as you walk down the street.

- ❧ MAKE a list of things to do to bring more kindness into the world and have a friend make a list. Exchange lists and do one item per day for a month.

- ❧ SPEND a week just being aware of things in nature that befriend you.

- ❧ OPEN the phone book and select a name at random and send that person a greeting card.

- ❧ HOLD a random acts of kindness party where everyone tells the stories of kindnesses in their life.

- ❧ WALK around with an Instamatic camera and take people's pictures and give them to them.

❧ BRING a little beauty into sterile places—drop off a geranium plant at a police station or a cutting from a houseplant to your local fire station.

❧ WHEN someone is trying to merge into your lane in traffic, let him in—and why not smile and wave while doing it!

❧ ALL of you reading these words have loved someone, have done someone a kindness, have healed a wound, have taken on a challenge, have created something beautiful, and have enjoyed breathing the air of existence. Never doubt how precious, how vitally important you are. Every moment you make a difference. So, today, appreciate yourself as a random act of kindness.

# The Secret Gardener

I moved into a new house a few years back. It was the first time I had a yard of any size. There was a small lawn, about thirty rosebushes, six camellias, five rhododendrons, and numerous smaller plants which, at the time, I could not even name. I was a bit overwhelmed and not doing a very good job of maintenance—especially of cutting the grass.

After a few weeks, I noticed—vaguely—that something seemed different when I came home one evening. But I didn't pay too much attention. Then one day I came home to find freshly cut grass, precisely trimmed around the edges, all around the sidewalks and driveway. I realized that someone had been weeding and pruning almost every day while I was away at work. Finally I caught the culprit in the act—my eighty-six-year-old neighbor, Mr. Okumoto. It's now been seven years and he's still doing it, not only my yard but the one behind his house and the one on the other side of his.

He's now ninety-three and I don't know how long I'll be blessed with his diligent work. Maybe forever.

......................

I am done with great things and big plans, great institutions and big success. I am for those tiny, invisible loving human forces that work from individual to individual, creeping through the crannies of the world like so many rootlets, or like the capillary oozing of water, which, if given time, will rend the hardest monuments of pride.

—*William James*

......................

People say that what we're all seeking is a meaning for life. . . . I think that what we're really seeking is an experience of being alive, so that our life experiences on the purely physical plane will have resonance within our innermost being and reality, so that we can actually feel the rapture of being alive.

—*Joseph Campbell*

# An Unexpected Apology

I was driving home from work one day and the traffic was terrible. We were crawling along and out of nowhere this guy just pulls out onto the shoulder, passes a whole line of cars, and cuts me off so quickly I have to slam on the brakes to keep from crashing into him. I was really rattled. About fifteen minutes later, I'm stopped at a light and I look over and there is the same guy next to me, waving for me to roll down my window. I could feel my adrenaline starting to flow and all my defenses coming up, but for some reason I roll down the window, and he says, "I am terribly sorry. Sometimes when I get into my car I become such a jerk. I know this must seem stupid, but I am glad I could find you to apologize." Suddenly my whole body just relaxed and all the tension and frustration of the day, the traffic, life just dissipated in this wonderfully warm, unexpected embrace.

......................

Compassion is an alternate perception.

—*M. C. Richards*

# Amazing Grace

We had just searched a small village that had been suspected of harboring Viet Cong. We really tore the place up—it wasn't hard to do—but had found nothing. Just up the trail from the village we were ambushed. I got hit and don't remember anything more until I woke up with a very old Vietnamese woman leaning over me. Before I passed out again I remembered seeing her in the village we had just destroyed and I knew I was going to die. When I woke again, the hole in my left side had been cleaned and bandaged, and the woman was leaning over me again offering me a cup of warm tea. As I was drinking the tea and wondering why I was still alive, a helicopter landed nearby to take me back. The woman quietly got up and disappeared down the trail.

......................

What good will it do you to think, "Oh, I have done evil, I have made many mistakes"? It requires no ghost to tell us that. Bring in the light, and the evil goes out in a moment.

—*Vivekananda*

# The Mentor

It was a blustery day in Pasadena, California. The year was 1970. I had just started the second quarter of my first year in the seminary. Sitting in Greek class one evening I realized I had to quit; I had no heart for the study of classic languages and philosophical theology. The next morning, amid the protestations of the registrar and my adviser, I filled out the forms to drop out of graduate school. I had been doing very well and no one understood why I was leaving. But I felt increasingly clear about the rightness of the decision.

As I was walking between the registrar's office and the library, I passed the office of one of my professors. He was sitting at his desk, noticed my passing, and called me into his office. He wondered about the forms I was carrying and inquired about what I was doing. I shared with him my decision to drop out and he very graciously responded with his disappointment and his blessing. Then he said something that eventually changed my life. Very kindly he remarked, "You are a talented young man with a future in theology, and even if you don't decide to go into the ministry, I think you should come back to complete your degree someday." I thanked him and walked out, quite touched by his kindness.

His prophecy came true. I returned two years later, completed my degree, found my way into theological publishing, and eventually the professor who had been so kind to me became one of my bestselling authors.

......................

I don't know what your destiny will be, but one thing I do know: the only ones among you who will be really happy are those who have sought and found how to serve.

—*Albert Schweitzer*

......................

Love is not getting, but giving. Not a wild dream of pleasure and a madness of desire—oh, no—love is not that! It is goodness and honor and peace and pure living— yes, love is that and it is the best thing in the world and the thing that lives the longest.

—*Henry Van Dyke*

# Don't Give Up

I had been stuck for years in a place that refused to change. Everything seemed hard, solid, and unmovable. Making the most difficult and painful decision of my life, I left the woman I had shared my life with for fourteen years—and started an avalanche of change that forced me down a dark and anguished path of sadness and growth. Every time I thought I had reached the bottom, another trapdoor would open below me. I had spent almost a year jettisoning useless baggage until I felt stripped raw, empty-handed, and emotionally exhausted.

The one tangible thing I had done was to buy a new car—a nice one—a car that was soft and comfortable and responsive. I was sinking, but I was trying to find a way out. One night I woke up in a cold sweat from a devastating nightmare. In the dream everything had been taken from me. In the last scene I stood on a street corner watching my car being driven away, knowing that I had nothing left and no way to go on.

The next morning as I dressed to go into San Francisco for a meeting, I was filled with foreboding. The dream clung to me and wouldn't let go. I arrived half an hour early and found a parking place right in front of the office I was visiting. It was a beautiful fall morning and I decided to calm my nerves with a walk. I was carefully locking my briefcase in the trunk when I was approached by a very polite, elderly Chinese man who was completely lost. I spread his map over the trunk of my car, showed him where he was, and traced the best route to his destination for him on the map.

He thanked me profusely and headed off. That small exchange boosted my spirits considerably and helped to dissipate the cloud of impending doom. First a perfect parking place, then a simple but honest human interaction. I put a dime in the parking meter and, after registering my ten minutes, the dime fell out of the empty cash-box hole and back into my hand; things were definitely looking up. I returned from my walk twenty minutes later and my car was gone. I reached in my pocket but my keys were not there—I had left them dangling from the lock on the trunk. The day unfolded like a bad dream. I called the police and they came to the wrong address. When they finally arrived I couldn't remember my license number (the plates had only been on the car for a week). I got a ride back home and spilled a full cup of coffee down my leg and into my shoe.

My ride dropped me off at the home of the woman I had left almost a year before. I had lent my old car to a close mutual friend who was staying with her, and I needed it back. I explained what had happened, and the woman I had loved for fourteen years looked at me and without a shred of compassion said, "Well, there's a message from the gods!" It pierced my heart like a knife. I knew she would regret having said it, but that no longer mattered.

That evening I stood outside on the deck of my house thinking about everything that was gone, everything that no longer mattered. Thinking that I never imagined life could be this painful or this lonely. Thinking how my self-support system had been reduced to driving my car, playing golf, and reading. And now my car was gone with my golf clubs and reading glasses safely locked in the trunk. I didn't know whether to laugh or cry so I did both. From behind me, inside the darkening house, I could hear music, Kate Bush singing the haunting refrain to Peter Gabriel's cry of despair: Don't give up . . . don't give up. . . . In front of me the sky bled a breathtaking deep purple-red sunset. I stood there watching the sunset dissolve into a stunningly beautiful and clear night. I knew that for all I had lost, I had lost nothing.

That night I went to bed exhausted but at peace for the first time in many, many months. I was awakened at midnight by a night-shift dispatcher for the San Francisco police department. My car and everything in it had been recovered undamaged.

. . . . . . . . . . . . . . . . . . . . . .

Living the truth in your heart without compromise brings kindness into the world. Attempts at kindness that compromise your heart cause only sadness.

—*Anonymous 18th-century monk*

# Who Was That Masked Woman?

I was at my sister's house, and I was there to rest. She lives in a big fancy house on the outskirts of Denver. All around her house is a canal. It's very safe, so I thought I would go for a little run—that's putting it too strongly—a little amble along the canal. I put on my little ambling shoes and started walking. All of a sudden, two women came running up the canal, screaming, "He's back there, he's back there, he's back there."

I have no idea why I did this, but I took one, two, three steps in the direction they were pointing and here comes this stark naked man with an erection running toward me. Without thinking, I let loose with an ear-piercing yell in the loudest voice I can, and he stops in mid-stride. I mean totally stops. Here I am, a woman standing there looking fiercely determined, and he stops, turns, and runs in the other direction. Then I went to the women who were still hysterical and helped them calm down. The man hadn't touched or hurt them. Finally I flagged down a trucker, and as the trucker called the police on his CB, I disappeared. I'm sure those two women were wondering, who was that masked woman?

........................

What you deny to others will be denied to you, for the plain reason that you are always legislating for yourself; all your words and actions define the world you want to live in.

—*Thaddeus Golas*

........................

A human being is a part of the whole that we call the universe, a part limited in time and space. He experiences himself, his thoughts and feelings, as something separated from the rest—a kind of optical illusion of his consciousness. This illusion is a prison for us, restricting us to our personal desires and to affection for only the few people nearest us. Our task must be to free ourselves from this prison by widening our circle of compassion to embrace all living beings and all of nature.

—*Albert Einstein*

# The Rescue

I was heading with my girlfriend through the Santa Cruz mountains on the way to a Samoyed breeder to pick up a new puppy. It was raining hard and the dirt road that was supposed to lead directly to the breeder's farmhouse was now simply a wide rut. My Honda was having more and more trouble with the mud and the steep incline, and there was an ugly drop into a now-rushing creek bed to one side of the road. Suddenly we ground to a complete stop: in the dark, stuck in heavy mud, with no tools, phones, or—so far as we knew—humans for miles.

We waited for about an hour, debating the merits of hiking in the pouring rain back toward civilization (miles away), trying to get the car unstuck (our attempts so far had just wedged us more firmly in the muck), and yelling (very, very loudly) for help. We were sitting in the car feeling hopeless when we saw faint lights behind us—we hadn't heard the engine because of the rain.

A young man in a VW stopped. He was headed past us on the hill toward his home beyond the breeder's farm. He told us he had towing equipment and would come back and get us unstuck, and would also let the breeder know we were still on the way. We settled back to wait, half doubting that he would return. After all, it was pouring, it was now 10:30 at night, and if he came back to do what he had promised, he'd be completely covered in mud within minutes. In forty-five minutes he was back with a truck and towing equipment. Half an hour later we sat in a warm kitchen, out of the rain, with hot cups of tea, surrounded by teacup-sized Samoyeds.

......................

Kindness is more important than wisdom, and the recognition of this is the beginning of wisdom.

—*Theodore Isaac Rubin*

# Pass It On

During the Depression my grandmother was a society matron in Cleveland and, as she put it, "quite taken with myself." One morning she found a basket of food on her doorstep. It made her furious—how could anyone think that she was some poor needy person? Not knowing what to do, she put the basket in the kitchen without even bothering to unpack it. The next morning another basket of food was on her front step. By the end of the week she had five food baskets beginning to clutter up her immaculate kitchen, and she decided that the least she could do was to pass the food along to those who were really needy. The baskets continued to arrive for a couple more weeks, and my grandmother realized that she had begun to look forward to her part in helping find someone who needed them. When the morning deliveries finally stopped, she starting making her own food baskets to give away.

The moral of the story? Said my grandmother, "Someone knew I really was a poor needy person and found the best way possible to help me."

# Seeing the Sky

I live high in the hills and my body is getting old. One day I was out in my garden fussing with weeds and grew tired. I decided to lie back on the grass and rest like I used to when I was a small boy. I woke up some minutes later with a neighbor whom I had never met leaning over me, all out of breath, asking me if I were OK. He had looked out his window two blocks up the hill and saw me lying on my back on the grass, looking, I am sure, like the victim of a stroke or heart attack, and had run all the way down the hill to check on me. It was embarrassing but it was also so wonderfully touching. After we had it all sorted out, he let out a deep breath and lay down on the grass beside me. We both stayed there very quietly for a while and then he said, "Thank you for deciding to take your nap out on the lawn where I could see you. The sky is such a beautiful thing and I cannot remember the last time I really looked at it."

# The Choice

I have a friend who lives in a small village in Austria. She will be eighty next March. During the war her husband, a simple, uneducated Catholic farmer, decided he couldn't serve in Hitler's army because it would be an immoral act. My friend, Franziska, supported his decision even though they were desperately in love. Eventually, he was convicted of treason and condemned to death. The day before his execution, Franziska went to visit him for one last time in Brandenburg prison in Berlin. After watching him being cruelly hurled off a truck, hands and feet bound, she was led by two guards into a room with a long table and two chairs. As she and her husband began to sit across from each other, one of the guards moved the chairs so that when they were sitting, they would be barely able to reach their hands across the table and touch. After an unimaginable last conversation, it was time to part. The other guard offered to bring the prisoner out, and the heartless guard left. The second guard then turned away from the couple long enough for them to rush into a last embrace. Waiting until their sobs quieted somewhat, he then said quietly, "It's time to go." A token act of kindness for a Nazi soldier, perhaps, but that man gave them one more moment to experience an extraordinary love.

......................

A hundred times every day I remind myself that my inner and outer life depends on the labors of other men, living and dead, and that I must exert myself in order to give in the measure as I have received and am still receiving.

—*Albert Einstein*

......................

If you help others, you will be helped, perhaps tomorrow, perhaps in one hundred years, but you will be helped. Nature must pay off the debt. . . . It is a mathematical law and all life is mathematics.

—*Gurdjieff*

# The Taxi Driver

New York City is a great place to find kindness because it is always such a surprise. I was going to a trade show and my plane was delayed, so by the time I got to my hotel everyone I was suppose to meet had already left for the show. The concierge told me that if I walked around the block I could catch a shuttle. So I walked to the bus stop but the last shuttle had already gone. Then a young man standing on the sidewalk said, "The convention center isn't very far, it's only four blocks." So I started walking. But it wasn't only four blocks, and I walked and walked.

Suddenly it started getting dark, I was already an hour late for my meeting, and I found myself in the warehouse district, definitely the kind of place you don't want to be when you're all by yourself in New York. Eventually I saw a little light in the distance and started walking toward it. As I walked, a taxi cab drove past, then backed up and asked me where I was going. I told him and he said, "Get in. I'll take you there." By then I was really relieved, particularly when it turned out to be quite far to the convention center. To make the moment even sweeter, when the driver dropped me off—safely back among my friends—he wouldn't take any money from me.

........................

If someone comes to you asking for help, do not say in refusal, "Trust in God, HE will help." Rather, act as if there were no God, and no one to help except you.

—*Zaddik*

........................

Some day, after we have mastered the winds, the waves, the tides and, gravity we shall harness the energies of love. Then, for the second time in the history of the world, man will have discovered fire.

—*Teilhard de Chardin*

# PRACTICE
## RANDOM ACTS OF KINDNESS!

❧ WRITE a letter of appreciation to that which in nature has been a safe place for you.

❧ As you go about your day, why not pick up the trash you find on the sidewalk?

❧ WRITE a card thanking a service person for his or her care and leave it with your tip. Be sure to include a very specific acknowledgment: "I appreciate the careful way you cleaned the room without disturbing my things"; "Your smile as you served me dinner really made my day."

❧ IF you are in any of the helping professions, ask your clients to tell you their stories of random acts of kindness.

❧ GIVE another driver your parking spot.

❧ FOR one week, act on every single thought of generosity that arises spontaneously in your heart and notice what happens as a consequence.

❧ A traveling salesman we know always carries cracked corn in his car and scatters it for birds during the snowy winter months.

❧ ON Thanksgiving, call up everyone you know and ask them what they are thankful for so they can feel their own gratitude.

❧ TALK to people at work about one of your random acts of kindness and ask what one of theirs is. Disclosure stimulates us to do more by emphasizing the pleasure of giving with no strings attached.

# A Trip to the Post Office

Kindness is not always a straight line. I was traveling in Central America with a friend and we were looking for a post office. We were standing on the corner and did not know what the word in Spanish for "post office" was. Some kind soul could see we were confused and came up to us. We tried to explain what we were looking for and he said, "Oh yea, yea," and led us, with our backpacks on in the middle of the heat of the day, down all these little crooked streets. It seemed like we walked for miles. Finally, he pointed us toward a building without any name on it. But when we went in, it turned out not to be the post office.

When we came out and were again standing around looking lost, someone else came up and asked if she could help—she knew where the post office was. Again we headed off as she guided us to another building which also had no sign and which also turned out not to be the post office. At this point we decided that even though we didn't know where we were, we were not going to listen to anybody else. But then another person came up and said, "I can help you." We said, "No thank you," but he was very insistent. He actually grabbed me by the hand and dragged me through the streets. Circling around, we came back to the original corner where we had been standing when we began. The stranger pointed across the street and there was the post office.

. . . . . . . . . . . . . . . . . . . . . .

Let us not be satisfied with just giving money. Money is not enough, money can be got, but they need your hearts to love them. So, spread your love everywhere you go.

—*Mother Teresa*

. . . . . . . . . . . . . . . . . . . . . .

It is good to have an end to journey toward; but it is the journey that matters, in the end.

—*Ursula K. LeGuin*

# The Skiing Accident

When I was about 19 or 20, I was skiing down a mountain when I saw a woman who had fallen. She was clearly hurt and crying and trying to get up, but she couldn't. So I flagged down somebody to get the ski patrol and stayed with her, talking to her, holding her hand, touching her shoulder. It was the last run of the day; it was getting really cold and snowing hard. About a half hour later, the ski patrol showed up and took her down the mountain. I stayed with her because she was so scared. She kept saying, "I think there might be something wrong." I said, "Well there might be. I'll make sure you get the care you need." Finally the ambulance came and took her to the hospital. I guess her leg was broken in about four places. I never saw her again, but it was clear my presence was important to her. I know that's true.

......................

To receive everything, one must open one's hands and give.

—*Taisen Deshimaru*

# Two Flat Tires

I used to make an eighty-mile drive to visit my parents. One forty-mile stretch of the road is in the middle of nowhere. One day as I was driving alone along this barren patch, I saw a family on the side of the road with a flat tire. Normally I do not stop in such situations, but for some reason I felt the need to do so that day. The family was very relieved when I volunteered to drive them to a gas station about ten miles down the road to get help. I left them at the station because the attendant said he would take them back to their car and drove on my way. About twelve miles later I had a blowout. Since I couldn't change the tire myself, I was stranded and not sure what to do. But in only about ten minutes along came a car and it pulled over to offer help. It was the same family I had stopped for earlier that day!

. . . . . . . . . . . . . . . . . . . . . .

This only is charity,
to do all, all that we can.

—*John Donne*

# Words of Comfort

I was walking up Amsterdam Avenue in New York during a particularly dark time of my life. I had recently lost a lover, and the pressures of law school were gaining on me. The darkness in my heart must have come to the surface because as I walked by a destitute street person he turned to me and said, "It can't be that bad." Simple words that changed my life and brought the spirit back to my form.

. . . . . . . . . . . . . . . . . . . . . .

When we think we're separate, we lose power. Whenever I say "my," I have lost my power. Power is not *my* power. . . . It is only gainable as part of a larger whole. Then you communicate with the rest of yourself—which may be a tree. You, reciprocally, are moved by the universe. Whenever you shut down connectedness, you get depressed. . . . It's fearful to know we're connected to everything in the universe, because then we're responsible.

—*Glenda Taylor*

# A Smile Is Worth . . .

One day I was walking down the street and saw a small boy standing outside a video arcade, wistfully peering inside. I asked him if he needed a quarter and he nodded his head. His smile as I handed him the money was worth way more than twenty-five cents!

47

. . . . . . . . . . . . . . . . . . . . .

The person who doesn't fit in with our notions of who is worthy of our love—the bag lady at the corner, the strange old man who rides through town on a three-wheel bike all strung up with flags—is just the person who, by not fitting into our patterns, insists that we expand not only our views but also our capacity to love. Today, see if you can stretch your heart and expand your love so that it touches not only those to whom you can give it easily, but also to those who need it so much.

*—Daphne Rose Kingma*

AFP
3/2010

# Kindness from a Stranger

A few winters ago, I was at a particularly distressing dinner with a friend who was having a difficult time with her then boyfriend and was considering leaving him. I was getting very worked up because the man she was dating was a very close friend of mine and I was torn between loyalty to her and my friendship with him. She got so upset with me that while I was in the bathroom, she paid her half of the check and left.

I was dumbfounded and hurt and so I rushed outside in a weak attempt to reason with her. But she was out of sight and I was so confused that I began to walk without thinking toward the bus stop a few blocks away. I was so lost in my troubles that I started when I felt a hand on my shoulder. I whirled around and to my surprise, there was the waitress from the restaurant holding my purse and coat which I had left in the booth. Without a word, she handed me my belongings and gave me a hug. I burst into tears. She smiled and said, "I have been through that before, and I know how it is. Go home, take a hot bath, and watch *Casablanca* until you fall asleep." I laughed, thanked her, climbed onto the bus, and never saw her again.

......................

The mother who gives up her life for her children does them no kindness but rather burdens them with the legacy of a life unlived.

—*Janet Falldron*

......................

If you live for love you spread kindness and compassion everywhere you go. When you stop believing in your heart you are but a sterile vessel wandering in the wilderness.

—*Francis Hegmeyer*

# The Eye Opener

I was living in Chicago and going through what was a particularly cold winter both in my personal life and the outside temperature. One evening I was walking home from a bar where I had been drinking alone, feeling sorry for myself, when I saw a homeless man standing over an exhaust grate in front of a department store. He was wearing a filthy sport coat and approaching everyone who passed by for money.

I was too immersed in my own troubles to deal with him so I crossed the street. As I went by, I looked over and saw a businessman come out of the store and pull a ski parka out of a bag and hand it to the homeless man. For a moment both the man and I were frozen in time as the businessman turned and walked away. Then the man looked across the street at me. He shook his head slowly and I knew he was crying. It was the last time I have ever been able to disappear into my own sorrow.

# Connections through Cancer

My wife was dying of cancer. There were lots of non-random kindnesses in our lives. People who knew us did many ordinary and extraordinary things. But what touched many of us in our community happened early in my wife's struggle. We decided to have a water filtration system installed in our house to take the impurities out of the water. The plumber we contacted installed the system and wouldn't accept any payment. We found out later his father had died of cancer.

......................

There is a love like a small lamp, which goes out when the oil is consumed; or like a stream which dries up when it doesn't rain. But there is a love that is like a mighty spring gushing up out of the earth; it keeps flowing forever, and is inexhaustible.

—*Isaac of Nineveh*

# Music for the Soul

When I was going through a very difficult time, someone called me up and played piano music for me on my answering machine. It made me feel very loved—and I never discovered who had done it.

......................

Every human being is your counterpart. Every other human being possesses and embodies aspects of yourself: your dreams, your sorrows, your hope that your life will not turn out to be a dirty joke. For each of us there was a time when the world was young, a springtime of spirit that was later tested by the winters of discontent; and in the midst of each of our lives lies the haunting shadow of death. Therefore we are all quite alike; indeed at the core we are all one, all lost—and found—in the same mysterious enterprise that is life. Hold this in your heart as you go about your day, and the world will cease to be inhabited by strangers, and the burden of life itself will no longer be a process of loneliness.

—*Daphne Rose Kingma*

# Payback

I had an older neighbor who was very kind to me, a father figure really. After he died, I noticed that his yard had become completely overgrown; his widow was not physically able to do the gardening. So one morning, after I saw her leave for the day, I jumped the fence and put in a few hours of work. It was my way of paying him back for the care he had taken of me.

......................

It is one of the most beautiful compensations of life that no man can sincerely try to help another without helping himself.

—*Ralph Waldo Emerson*

AFP
04.15.10

# PRACTICE
## RANDOM ACTS OF KINDNESS!

❧ YOUR car is a place where you can make many courteous gestures with little effort. Sometimes smiling at the person in the car next to you or waving hello to a pedestrian in the crosswalk can really lift not only the other person's spirits, but your own.

❧ VISIT a neighbor with a bouquet of flowers for no reason at all.

❧ SEND a letter to a teacher you once had letting her know about the difference she made in your life.

❧ SAY "Thank you" to someone who helps you and really mean it. You might want to look into his eyes, smile, and, if he is wearing a name tag, say his name as well.

🐟 Buy a cold drink for your entire row at the baseball game.

🐟 Ask an older person to tell you a story about his or her youth, such as what her favorite song was and why, or how he met his spouse.

🐟 Let the person behind you in line at the grocery store go ahead of you.

🐟 Order a mail-order gift, anonymously, for a friend or someone at work who needs to be cheered up.

🐟 Take out an ad in your local weekly newspaper thanking a tree, a park, a stream, a sunset, for giving you comfort.

# In a Strange Town

It was on my first trip to the States. I arrived in New York as a student and went down to the bus station to buy a ticket. I had my money in one hand and my handbag in the other—it didn't have anything valuable but my address book in it. Going up to the counter to pay, I put my bag down for a second and when I looked again, it was gone. I couldn't believe it. I started to panic because I realized that without my address book I didn't know how to get in contact with my brother, with whom I was going to stay.

The friend who was with me suggested we go to the police. With what I knew about New York's reputation I told her that would be a waste of time. But we went anyway and met two policemen who seemed to be straight out of a television show. They couldn't have been nicer. They said, "Such a terrible thing to happen to you on your first trip to America." They took down the details and then started asking me questions, "Where was I going?" "Did I know how to get in touch with my brother?" Of course I didn't because my address book was gone. Then one policeman said, "Do you know anybody who knows him?" And I remembered I knew his in-laws. So they allowed me to make a long-distance phone call to the in-laws to get my brother's address and phone number. And when I got off the phone they said I should go ahead and call my brother right then and there so I wouldn't be anxious. Then they walked us back to the bus stop where we could find our way back to our hotel.

........................

The beginning and end of Torah is performing acts of loving kindness.

—The Talmud

........................

The question is not whether we will die, but how we will live.

—*Joan Borysenko*

# Corporate Kindness

I am a corporate lawyer, and several years ago I was at my first closing. The investment banker came to deliver a check for $55 million to my client, and before my client arrived, I went to the Xerox machine to copy the check for our records. I put the check in the feeder of the copier, and it promptly shredded it! I told the banker about the mutilated check, and a moment later my client arrived, eager to receive the money. The banker looked at me and said to the client, "I can't believe it! I forgot the check!" He left and returned an hour later with a new check, and I kept my job.

......................

Our lives are fed by kind words and gracious behavior. We are nourished by expressions like "Excuse me," and other such simple courtesies. . . . Rudeness, the absence of the sacrament of consideration, is but another mark that our time-is-money society is lacking in spirituality, if not also in its enjoyment of life.

—*Ed Hays*

# The Car Angel

I had just quit a job I hated and was determined to find a way to live that felt right. Money was very tight and my car was dying on me—I mean really falling apart. A friend gave me the name of a guy who lived close to me and fixed cars. So I took my wreck to him and he fixed it. I mean he fixed everything—working on it for two days and charging me only $60. The parts alone had to have cost him quite a bit more than that! It was almost as though he read into my soul: "This girl doesn't have money, and she needs this car." He didn't know me from Adam. That car was my vehicle for getting to where I needed to go and this total stranger made that possible when I really needed it.

. . . . . . . . . . . . . . . . . . . . . .

Through our willingness to help others we can learn to be happy rather than depressed.

—*Gerald Jampolsky*

# Dusty, the Horse

My husband and I travel a lot, and at the time this happened I had a horse, a wonderful horse. We were out of town when a one-hundred-mile endurance horse race (that's a race where people from all over New England get together and travel as fast as they can for one hundred miles) went right past our driveway. My horse, whose name was Dusty, decided that she wanted to join the race. So she jumped over the fence. Galloped off. No saddle. Nobody on her back.

The next day when my husband and I came home there was a note on the front door from the sheriff saying that my horse had gone back to the barn on the other side of town where she had been born eighteen years before. So we drove there. It was a lovely old farm, owned now by people I didn't know.

The new owners were a man, his wife, and their children, two little girls ages seven and five. And sure enough there in the corral behind the barn were the two girls and Dusty. The man told me that that morning when they had gotten up, the little girls had started screaming because at the top of the hill, with the sun rising behind her, was this beautiful palomino horse. They lured her into their corral and proceeded to spend the day brushing her and treating her a lot better than she had been for many years under my sometimes care.

They looked so happy. The seven-year-old girl turned and, with a trembling lip, said, "Can I ride her before you take her back?" I said that she could have her for another half-hour or so. And then I went to the local general store and bought a bottle of apple cider. When I returned, they told me they had always wished for a horse but their parents really didn't have the money for one. I sat them down and told them I was going to give them Dusty. And that I wanted them to promise me that someday when they were grown up they each would find a little girl and give her—a little girl they didn't know—some very special gift that she had always wanted.

Then we celebrated with a bubbling glass of apple cider, toasting to Dusty.

......................

Give light, and the darkness will disappear of itself.

*—Erasmus*

......................

The heart that breaks open can contain the whole universe.

*—Joanna Macy*

......................

We who lived in concentration camps can remember the men who walked through the huts comforting others, giving away their last piece of bread. They may have been few in number, but they offer sufficient proof that everything can be taken away from a man but one thing: the last of the human freedoms—to choose one's attitude in any given set of circumstances, to choose one's own way.

*—Viktor Frankl*

6/20/10
AFP

# Competitive Kindness

When I was in high school, I started playing field hockey. Since this was on the West Coast, there were no organized men's leagues, and we would more often than not end up playing college teams or adult club teams. One day we played the local university team which included one of the best field hockey players in the country. They killed us. I remember running around like mad, exerting massive amounts of energy while this one guy just glided around, past, and through us to score whenever he wanted. After the game I was sitting on the ground trying to catch my breath when the star walked over and started talking to me. For a while he just talked, going into all the intricacies of the game; he spoke to me as if I were an equal, as if I already understood all the things he was saying. After I had finally caught my breath, he took me back out on the field and spent an hour showing me various moves and tactics. I know it sounds silly, but even though the words were all about field hockey, the feeling it gave me was so much larger.

# Beyond Words

I was in Tokyo, at the main train station, trying to take the bullet train to Kyoto. The station is huge—there's more than fifty departure and arrival platforms and all the signs are in Japanese. No one I tried to get directions from spoke any English. The time I was supposed to depart was nearing and I had not yet found the correct platform. In a state of near panic, I went to a ticket window and explained my predicament to the agent, only to be met with his blank stare. Obviously, he spoke no English.

Pointing to my tickets and to my suitcases, I communicated my desperation to him in body language. Suddenly, his face showed signs of comprehension. Jumping across the counter, he grabbed one of my suitcases with one hand and my arm with the other and began to run. For the next five minutes or so, the ticket agent and I were engaged in a weird dance as we weaved across platforms, bridges, and alleys, through tunnels, and past crowded passages, suitcases in hand, to the one platform he knew was the right one. Literally seconds after I entered the car into which he pushed me and shoved the suitcases, the door closed and the train pulled out of the station.

. . . . . . . . . . . . . . . . . . . . . .

Experience praises the most happy the one who made the most people happy.

—*Karl Marx*

. . . . . . . . . . . . . . . . . . . . . .

Keep on sowing your seed, for you never know which will grow—perhaps it all will.

—*Ecclesiastes*

# Stranded

In the summer of 1977, a friend and I were driving in my 1967 VW bug to Ashland, Oregon, when my car threw a rod in the middle of nowhere on a Sunday (of course). We finally tracked down a tow truck driver who took the car to some swampy, willowy grove by the ocean—a wonderful place of rest, a kind of car heaven.

Meanwhile, however, we were completely stuck in this godforsaken place, at least until some means of transportation could be found when businesses opened up again on Monday. So the tow truck driver took us to his wonderful little woodsy home in the Mendocino mountains, fed us, and put us up for the night. Wonderful!

......................

Each small task of everyday life is part of the total harmony of the universe.

—*St. Thérèsa of Lisieux*

# Neighborly Kindness

For years, the Oakland, California, neighbors watched as Mary's house and yard slowly decayed. Mary was an elderly, wheelchair-bound widow who could no longer manage the necessary repairs and maintenance on her house. One day a couple of neighbors—a bus driver and an auto worker—went down to the city's Office of Community Development, got forty-five gallons of Mary's favorite-colored paint and a handful of painting supplies, and set to work. By the time they had finished, they had also put in a new lawn, cut back the tangled shrubs, and topped off the paint job with eye-catching trim.

. . . . . . . . . . . . . . . . . . . . . .

Little kindnesses . . . will broaden your heart, and slowly you will habituate yourself to helping your fellow man in many ways.

—*Zadik*

# Glasgow, Scotland

I was traveling by Britrail through England and Scotland and got caught on a weekend with no money. (I had a bank account but couldn't get any cash out until Monday.) I decided to ride an overnight train from London to Inverness on Sunday so I wouldn't have to worry about staying in a hotel; the next morning I could go to the bank and all would be fine. I didn't check the rail schedule very well, though, and the train I was on came to a dead end in Glasgow at one A.M.

At the time, Glasgow had a terribly rough reputation. I'd never been there and never wanted to be, but there I was with no money and nowhere to go. For some reason (exhaustion? innocence?), instead of just staying on a bench in the train station till morning, I picked up all my bags and started walking down the streets of Glasgow.

The story could have ended pretty badly. There were gangs of what looked like thugs on every corner, and here was I, a twenty-something, American woman who obviously had nowhere to go. But then a policeman came along. He took me to a nearby YWCA, talked the matron into letting me stay (it was a shelter for battered wives and didn't really take in tourists), and even paid the fee when I told him I didn't have any money! The next morning, I went to the bank, walked to the police station, and left it for him. I'm sure he was surprised to get it, since he obviously thought I didn't really have any money. The kindness of that policeman and also the women in the shelter who gave me breakfast and let me take a shower and wash my clothes made me think Glasgow was a very friendly place!

..........................

It is in the shelter of each other that the people live.

—*Irish proverb*

..........................

Our deeds determine us, as much as we determine our deeds.

—*George Eliot*

# Kindness of Strangers

We were traveling in Prague, one of the most confusing cities in Europe. It was nighttime and we were in a large rented car, utterly lost, finding our considerable German, moderate French, and hopeful English unusable on any storekeeper or street-corner policeman. The street signs were all painted on dark brown metal and averaged about fifteen letters, all consonants. At one point we found ourselves at the end of a dead end—Czech mate!

Finally we found ourselves in the middle of a pedestrian mall with nowhere to go, wondering if we should just pull over and spend the night in the car. A man and his wife appeared. We tried German once more and this time it worked. We asked directions to Wenceslaus Platz. He started explaining at length until his wife pulled at his sleeve and said, "You can't get there from here. Get in and show them." So he got in our car, she in theirs, and they accompanied us through a considerable section of Prague to the door of our hotel, at which point they wished us a cordial good night. We never saw them again, but were safe in a strange city thanks to the kindness of strangers.

......................

Love and pity and wish well to every soul in the world; dwell in love, and then you dwell in God; hate nothing but the evil that stirs in your own heart.

—*William Law*

......................

Whenever you are to do a thing, though it can never be known but to yourself, ask yourself how you would act were all the world looking at you and act accordingly.

—*Thomas Jefferson*

# A Cup of Coffee

My grandmother was born in Russia at a time of great confusion and instability. She emigrated to this country as a young girl and ended up marrying a man who was extraordinarily successful. She could have lived in the fanciest neighborhood and eaten only at the best restaurants; instead she lived in a very modest area and would go to Woolworth's for coffee. In those days, a cup of coffee cost five cents, and whenever my grandmother would buy a cup, she would always leave a five-dollar tip. Her explanation was simple: "They work hard for their money."

........................

True kindness presupposed the faculty of imagining as one's own the suffering and joy of others.

—*Andre Gide*

# City Kindness

I was about to go into the hospital to be operated on for breast cancer when there was a knock on my door. It was a man from the utility company telling me that the next week they were going to tear up the street in front of my house to put in a new sewer. My face fell and I said, "This is terrible! I'll just be back from the hospital convalescing from cancer surgery." The man turned and left. I later found out that they totally rearranged their schedule so that the work on my street wouldn't begin till several weeks later to give me some peace and quiet when I first got home! For years later, I would see that guy working on the sewers around town and we'd wave to one another.

. . . . . . . . . . . . . . . . . . . . . .

Tenderness and kindness are not signs of weakness and despair but manifestations of strength and resolution.

—*Kahlil Gibran*

# In the Grocery Store

The other day I went with a friend to the grocery store to buy a few things, and we were standing in the express line which, as usual, was about a block long. In front of us was a woman with a gallon of milk and a loaf of bread who was muttering under her breath about how disgraceful it was that she had to wait so long, how the store never had enough checkers, how express was supposed to mean fast, how the clerk wasn't supposed to let people use checks and she could see him cashing a check for some idiot who couldn't even read the sign— it was a constant monologue all the way up to the checkstand.

When she finally arrived, the clerk rang up her total as just over $4; reaching into her purse, she discovered she had no money. She just stopped dead with an incredulous expression on her face. I was just standing there transfixed when my friend reached over, handed the clerk a $5 bill, and said, "I'll pay for it." I hope the incident makes her future waits a little easier to endure.

# Give and You Shall Receive

I'm a doctor. Every day I come into the office and, probably like most doctors, slip into my professional caring role. I try hard to always be in a positive and attentive frame of mind for each and every one of my patients. But every now and then one of my patients will turn the tables on me and it is always such a genuinely touching thing. There I am, figuratively leaning forward, ready to be the one to do the giving, and out comes a bag of vegetables fresh from the garden, a coffee cake, a bouquet of home-grown flowers. The turnaround—the receiver giving to the giver—never fails to take me by surprise and always puts a large goofy grin on my face.

. . . . . . . . . . . . . . . . . . . . . .

Kind words can be short and easy to speak but their echoes are truly endless.

—*Mother Teresa*

# PRACTICE
## RANDOM ACTS OF KINDNESS!

❦ BUY a big box of donuts or chocolates for the office next to yours. Or the kids who hang out on the street corner. Or the UPS person or the mail carrier.

❦ MAKE an anonymous donation to some local charity that is actively helping people—feeding the homeless, providing foster care for children, and so on. Or start a fund-raising drive in your office for such organizations.

❦ BAKE a cherry pie and leave it on someone's doorstep.

❦ SLIP a $20 bill into the pocketbook of a needy friend (or stranger).

❦ ORGANIZE your friends and workmates to gather their old clothes and give them to homeless people.

🕭 Get a big piece of paper and a magic marker, and sit back to back with a friend. Across the top of the page, write the words physical, emotional, aesthetic, spiritual, and relational. Set an alarm clock for ten minutes and make a thank-you card for all the people, places, or things that have affected you in those dimensions. When the time is up, share your paper with one another.

🕭 Go to an AIDS hospice or hospital ward and see what you can do for one person.

🕭 Next time you go over a toll bridge pay the toll for the car behind you and don't forget to thank the toll taker.

# Gifts from the Angels

I was in Los Angeles visiting my father who was in the hospital. He had gone into a coma and my sister and I had gone there expecting to say good-bye to him. But he had revived.

It had been quite an ordeal emotionally, dealing with the hospital atmosphere with the thought my father was dying, and then the relief when he came out of the coma. As we were leaving the hospital, we had to cross a courtyard and this tiny little girl—she couldn't have been more than fifteen months old—came running over to me with a beautiful bouquet of pink and purple flowers in her hand. She held out her arm to show me the flowers. I bent down to smell them and she put them into my hand. When I took the flowers, she stepped back, got a huge smile on her face, and clapped her hands. It was like a gift from the angels.

......................

Let the beauty we love be what we do.

*—Rumi*

# Ice Cream, Ice Cream!

It was one of those ice-cream days of summer. The kind where it gets so hot that you are almost literally pulled down to the ice-cream parlor. When I found myself there this particularly steamy day, it was an ice-cream zoo—people standing in a line that ran out the door, people standing around the front eating ice cream, people wandering down the street, ice cream in hand. After waiting patiently for what seemed like forever, I finally got my double scoop of strawberry (I never was all that adventurous about ice cream). As I turned to leave, I came across a small boy standing in the doorway with an empty sugar cone in his hand and two scoops of strawberry melting away on the sidewalk. He had giant tears streaming down his cheeks and his mother was saying, "You should have been more careful." I took one look at his double scoop of strawberry on the sidewalk and my double scoop still neatly packed into a sugar cone, handed it to him, and walked away.

# The Turn Around

I had just completed my training as a chiropractor and I wanted to open an office. Then the perfect place just fell into my lap, but I did not have any money. None. And I needed not only rent money, but money for a table, chairs, and so forth. I called a few friends but was only able to raise around a thousand dollars total—not nearly enough. Then I got a call from a man who was the cook at the school where I had trained. He told me to stop by because he had something for me. When I went over, he led me into the back room of the kitchen. There on a table was a large stack of money. Handing me a piece of paper and a pen, he told me to count the money and write up an IOU. It was around $6,000—an unbelievably trusting and generous gift. After getting my office set up and beginning my practice, things suddenly started going very badly. Within a few months nine friends and relatives of mine died. Here I was trying to build a practice at the same time that I was being overwhelmed by grief and working under the added pressure that it was someone else's money I was working with. As a result the practice was not going well and I was rapidly approaching bankruptcy.

One day I woke up, went into the office, and decided that something good had to happen. So I gave my secretary a raise. She said, "You can't afford to do that," but I told her I couldn't afford not to. That day everything began to turn around and I was eventually able to pay back the cook.

......................

He alone is great who turns the voice of the wind into a song made sweeter by his own loving.

—*Kahlil Gibran*

......................

Let us be kinder to one another.

—*Aldous Huxley,*
*on his deathbed*

# Courageous Kindness

An act of kindness can sometimes take incredible courage. I was at the county fair many years ago with my mother. I remember it was a very, very hot day and all around us children and parents were melting down. We were walking behind a woman with two small children. The children were crying and whining and the mother was getting increasingly upset. Finally she started to scream at them to shut up; then she turned around and struck them both very hard. Just to see this happen right in front of me made me feel like I had been hit as well.

Of course her kids starting crying even more and the mother was on the verge of completely losing control when my mother walked up to her, touched her arm, and said something like, "You poor dear, don't worry, sometimes things just get out of control for a moment." Then my mother offered to take the children over to the ice-cream stand, buy them some ice cream, and sit with them while the woman took a little walk to compose herself. She returned in about ten minutes, thanked my mother, hugged her children, and went on.

......................

The best portions of a good man's life,
His little, nameless, unremembered acts,
Of kindness and love.

—*William Wordsworth*

......................

Life is short and we have never too much time for gladdening the hearts of those who are travelling the dark journey with us. Oh be swift to love, make haste to be kind.

—*Henri Frederick Amiel*

# Roadside Service

We were on vacation in Florida, with four kids all under the age of ten. The weather had been very hot and humid so this particular day we decided to pack a cooler full of sandwiches and soft drinks and drive out along the coast until we found a nice beach. It was sort of an adventure since we really didn't know where we were going, but after a while we found a really beautiful beach that was pretty isolated. We parked and unloaded ourselves onto the sand. It was really great, except that, after a few hours, it just got too hot for the kids and they were starting to whine and complain. So we decided to head back to the air-conditioned hotel. When we got back to the car, however, there were the keys, dangling from the ignition with all the windows rolled up and all the doors locked. In frustration I screamed, "Who locked the doors?" to which Beth, my five-year-old, responded, "You tell us always to lock the doors." I felt totally defeated. At first I was just going to smash the window in, but after Beth's evenhanded comment, I thought that would be a bit too violent. So I walked up the road about a half-mile to a house along the beach. When I got there, this elderly couple invited me in, let me use their telephone to call roadside service, then packed me into their car and drove back to pick up the rest of my family. They brought us all back to their home, and within a few minutes the kids were swimming in their pool while my wife and I sat on an air-conditioned veranda sipping a cool drink and swapping vacation stories. Roadside service came and went and three hours later we headed back to our hotel, much refreshed and glowing from the surprising and wonderful experience.

......................

When strangers start acting like neighbors . . . communities are reinvigorated.

—*Ralph Nader*

......................

It is better to give and receive.

—*Bernard Gunther*

# Unknown Connections

One cold September day, a friend and I decided to eat lunch together downtown before heading back to our respective suburbs. As we made our way down the steps to the restaurant entrance, we spied a young mother off to one side, trying to corral the energy of her toddler in the middle of a tantrum. I was struck by the energy of the child's cry and the writhing movements of her body. The mother was struggling too, trying to give her daughter some space to vent safely without making too much of a spectacle. As the mother of a six-year-old myself, I could relate.

We walked on past, went into the restaurant, and were promptly seated. But the scene I had just witnessed would not leave my mind. I had barely sat down before I stood again, telling my friend that I was going to see what I could do for the mom. Stepping outside, I reached out my hand to touch the troubled mother's arm and asked, "Are you all right?" The young woman was clearly surprised. She was holding her somewhat-settled crying daughter on her lap and things had more or less run their course. "Do you have kids?" she asked. Then, as her daughter climbed up and down the stairs, we shared stories, frustrations, favorite ways to cope with our children's seemingly boundless energy. It was quite a few minutes into the conversation before we introduced ourselves and discovered to our amazement that we lived just four blocks from each other in the same small town.

..........................

Do everything with a mind that lets go. Do not expect praise or reward.

—*Achaan Chah*

..........................

A knowledge of the path cannot be substituted for putting one foot in front of the other.

—*M. C. Richards*

# The Good Friend

A good friend and I had finally gotten together one evening after months of trying to make our schedules and the fifty miles separating us fit together somehow. We went out to eat and as usual had a great time talking about everything. I am always amazed at how quickly and deeply we reconnect even after months of barely speaking on the telephone.

While we were catching up on each other's lives, she noticed a man sitting alone at a table in the corner of the restaurant and commented to me that he looked sad, as if he were lacking for company. When we had finished our meal, I insisted on paying and my friend went along smiling. When the waiter came to pick up the check, my friend told him that she would like to pay—anonymously—for the dinner of the man in the corner. I realized again why I cared about her so much.

. . . . . . . . . . . . . . . . . . . . .

No joy can equal the joy of serving others.

—*Sai Baba*

# Trust

This is a story that's about fifty years old. During World War II, my father-in-law and his pregnant wife, who were living in Texas, wanted to visit with his parents in Oklahoma before he went to the Philippines. They had to drive back roads all the way. To their dismay, they had a flat and no spare tire. Walking several deserted miles, they finally came to a farmhouse. Now this was in the days when rubber was rationed, but the farmer who lived there took off a tire from his car and said, "Drive into town, get your tire fixed, and leave mine at the gas station. I'll get my tire back later on." His trusting action really saved the day for my in-laws.

......................

I try to give to the poor people for love what the rich could get for money. No. I wouldn't touch a leper for a thousand pounds, yet I willingly cure him for the love of God.

—*Mother Teresa*

# PRACTICE
## RANDOM ACTS OF KINDNESS!

❧ IF someone in your neighborhood leaves on a trip and forgets to stop the newspaper, pick them up and put them in a safe out-of-view spot.

❧ NEXT time you go to the movies, pick out someone behind you in the line and tell the ticket seller you want to pay for their ticket as well. Make sure to ask that they not reveal who paid for their ticket.

❧ IF you have any artistic abilities, buy a shopping bag full of art supplies and take it and yourself out to a playground or recreation center in a poor neighborhood and go to it.

❧ IF you know someone who is going through a bad day or a difficult time in life, make it better by doing something—anything—to let him or her know someone cares . . . and don't let on who did it!

☙ LAUGH out loud often and share your smile generously.

☙ PRAISE the work or attitude of a person you work with to someone else in the office in a time, place, and manner that is outside of all office politics.

☙ IF you are the boss, bring your secretary a cup of coffee in the morning.

☙ BUY gift certificates—for a kids' clothing store, a record store, whatever suits your mood—and find a way to get them—anonymously—to people you think could really use them.

# The Baseball Mitt

When I was in college, I worked part-time at a sporting goods store. There was a kid who would come by two or three times a week to visit with this baseball mitt that he wanted to buy. My manager and I would joke about him not only because he was so dedicated and persistent, but also because he had picked the best and most expensive mitt in the shop to get obsessed about.

This went on for months. The kid would come in, and you could tell he was so relieved that the mitt was still there. He would put it on, pound his fist into the pocket a couple of times, and then very carefully put it back onto the shelf and leave. Finally, one day he came in with a shoe box and a smile about eight miles wide and announced that he wanted to buy the mitt. So the manager brought the mitt over to the cash register while the kid counted out a shoe box worth of nickels, quarters, and dimes. His stash came to exactly $19.98.

The mitt cost $79.98, not including tax. My manager looked at the price tag, and sure enough the 7 was a little smudged, enough that a desperately hopeful seven-year-old could imagine it to be a 1. Then he looked at me, smiled, and very carefully recounted. "Yep, exactly $19.98." Wrapping up the mitt, he gave it to the boy.

......................

Shall we make a new rule of life from tonight: always to try to be a little kinder than is necessary.

—*Sir James M. Barrie*

......................

T'was a thief said the last kind word to Christ.
Christ took the kindness and forgave the theft.

—*Robert Browning*

# The Hills of San Francisco

You hear stories about tourists trying to drive in San Francisco all the time. I discovered a whole new twist one day when I was walking up a particularly steep hill and saw a car stopped near the top with a very frightened woman inside. As I watched, she made a few attempts to get moving but each time seemed to lose more ground than she gained. Then a man came out of the corner market. The next thing I know, she gets out of the car and goes around to the passenger side while he climbs into the driver's seat and promptly drives the car up over the top of the dreaded hill. By then, I had reached the store where the helpful man's wife was standing, watching the proceedings. She told me that her husband, who owns the market, has been doing that for years, and that during the summertime—peak tourist season—he will "rescue" as many as ten scared drivers a week.

........................

Miracles occur naturally as expressions of love. The real miracle is the love that inspires them. In this sense everything that comes from love is a miracle.

—A Course in Miracles

........................

Charity is in the heart of man, and righteousness is the path for men. Pity the man who has lost his path and does not follow it and who has lost his heart and does not know how to recover it. When people's dogs and chicks are lost they go out and look for them and yet the people who have lost their hearts do not go out and look for them. The principle of self-cultivation consists in nothing but trying to look for the lost heart.

—Mencius

# Tree Climbing

One day when I was a senior in high school, I was walking home from school and noticed an elderly couple standing at the base of a very tall pine tree. They were looking up and yelling and they were obviously very upset. I thought that maybe their cat had gotten stuck in the tree, and since I had spent many of my best times as a young boy climbing trees, I went to see if I could help.

At the top of the tree was a very young girl. She couldn't have been more than three or four years old. Apparently she was staying with her grandparents and, when they weren't looking, had shimmied up the tree. They had already called the fire department, but I felt like I should at least climb up far enough so that if she started to fall I might be able to catch her. When I got within a few feet of the little girl, she gave me this huge smile and said "Hi." I almost started laughing because she was not at all scared; in fact she looked as much at ease as a monkey on its home branch. We ended up talking for a while about how great it felt to climb trees, and as we talked, cradled in that pine tree, I could feel my whole body relaxing into the tree. I had this wonderful feeling that everything was just right with the world.

Then she said, "We better go down now," and, as we climbed down the tree (I was very careful to keep myself close and below her), I could see that she was never in any real danger. She moved as though she could scramble up and down that tree a million times and never come close to slipping. As I walked home, I realized that that was the first time I had crawled out onto the limb of a tree in many, many years. The thought made me want to go back and thank that little girl.

.....................

If you stop to be kind, you must swerve often from your path.

—*Mary Webb*

......................

Wherever there is a human being there is an opportunity for kindness.

—*Seneca*

......................

May it be, oh Lord, That I seek not so much to be consoled as to console, to be understood as to understand, to be loved as to love. Because it is in giving oneself that one receives; it is in forgetting oneself that one is found; it is in pardoning that one obtains pardon.

—*St. Francis of Assisi*

# Weeping Willows

When I was in high school, I had a friend who asked me to help him plant some weeping willow trees down by a creek. It seems that he had watched every year as the banks of this creek had been increasingly eaten away. It had gotten to the point where the water was threatening to overflow into the nearby housing development. My friend had obviously done his research; he found out that willows grew quickly, easily, and with a great spreading root system that drinks up lots of water which would stabilize the creek bank. When I met him at the creek, he had a huge bundle of willow branches in his arms. We spent most of the day planting these willow sprigs up and down the endangered curve.

Many years later, I was home visiting and found myself walking down by that creek. Where we spent that afternoon is now a beautiful idyllic bend with a long curving row of large graceful willows bending out over the water.

# Winter Blues

February is not my time of year. I don't know if it is my own seasonal mood swings or just that my surroundings have such a big impact on me that after so many months of winter, my mood begins to resemble the dirty, slushy, gray world outside. I begin to walk around as if a dark cloud were inside my head. Everything looks gloomy and depressing.

A few years ago I was in the middle of a particularly depressing February and even though I had gone through this feeling many times before and knew it would eventually pass, I had gotten to the point where I was beginning to believe it would never get better. It was a Friday and my children were off to visit their father for the weekend. I can remember thinking as I went to sleep that night that this time I would be stuck forever in winter. When I woke up there was an eerie silence all over the house. I walked over to the front door and opened it. Outside, the world had remade itself into the most sparkling, beautiful, and inviting place imaginable. A late-night snowstorm had covered everything with a soft pristine layer of white. The sun was up and shining brightly; everywhere I looked the snow was dancing with light. Suddenly all the dark clouds in my mind were gone and I started laughing. I must have looked like a crazy woman standing in my bathrobe at the front door, laughing out into the silent empty yard. It seemed like a great joke. Winter, the dark dreary tormentor of my soul, had pulled a fast one and slipped in a day of incredible purity and beauty just to remind me of the possibilities in life.

......................

There must be more to life than having everything!

—*Maurice Sendak*

......................

Give help rather than advice.

—*Luc de Vauvenargues*

# The Giant Oak Tree

I had just graduated from college and had gone back to the town I grew up in to visit friends. My parents had sold the family home a few years back and moved out of state so I also took the opportunity to drive by the old house just to see it. Out in the front yard, perched in "my" giant oak tree, was a boy about ten years old. I stopped the car, went over to introduce myself, and told the boy that when I was his age I practically lived in that tree. He though that was real funny because he said his mother was always telling people that he lives in that tree.

While we were standing there talking, laughing, and feeling very good about our shared tree, a car drove up to the curb right in front of us. A middle-aged man got out of the driver's side, came around to the passenger side, and helped a very frail-looking old man out of the car. I guess we were both staring, but the old man just walked right up to the tree, patted it on the side, looked at us, and said, "I planted this tree sixty years ago when there was nothing here but fields. I still like to come visit it now and then." Then he turned around, got back into the car, and drove away. We were both so shocked we didn't say a word until after the old man had left. Then the boy just looked at me and said, "Wow."

......................

Let us not be justices of the peace, but angels of peace.
—*St. Thérèsa of Lisieux*

......................

No man giveth, but with intention of good to himself; because gift is voluntary, and of all voluntary acts the object is to every man his own good.
—*Thomas Hobbes*

# The Trundle Bed

I had no money. I had made the heartbreaking decision to end my marriage of eight years and move out on my own. A friend had offered me the vacant bedroom in his apartment to be my nest while I got on my feet again. I had to be very selective about the things I could use in this very small space. And there wasn't just me to consider. My young son would be staying with me several nights a week. So the queen-sized bed I already owned was not a practical choice. I began looking through the want ads for a used trundle bed, so I could get two beds for the space of one. Asking prices ranged from $100 to $200 for the nice ones. Cheaper ones seemed to be gone by the time I picked up the phone.

One day I spoke to a good friend about my frustration and resignation about sleeping on the floor for a while. It just so happened that a wooden trundle bed was sitting on her front porch, a recent discard by one of the neighboring tenants. I picked it up and my son and I slept peacefully for months on it.

......................

The only gift is a portion of thyself. . . . The poet brings his
poem; the shepherd his lamb . . . the girl, a handkerchief
of her own sewing.

—*Ralph Waldo Emerson*

......................

Of neighborhoods, benevolence is the most beautiful.
How can the man be considered wise who when he had
the choice does not settle in benevolence.

—*Confucius*

# Service with a Smile

I was out to dinner with a friend and we ended up talking for a while with our waitress. She was one of those waitresses who was such a pleasure she made the whole dining experience that much more enjoyable. She told us about how she was working two jobs and trying to put herself through school at night.

It was not a very expensive restaurant, and I think our total bill was less than $20. But when we paid, we left her a $100 tip. What a great feeling.

........................

The great, dominant, all controlling fact of this life is the innate bias of the human spirit, not towards evil, as the theologists tell us, but towards good. But for that bias, man would never have been man; he would only have been one more species of wild animal ranging a savage, uncultivated globe, the reeking battleground of sheer instinct and appetite.

—*William Archer*

# Helping a Friend in Need

There was a time in my life when everything was working so smoothly, I found myself sitting at home one Saturday with all my work done, all my household chores completed: dishes washed, laundry folded and put away, house dusted, grocery shopping completed, and that delicious feeling of having nothing to do. Then I thought about a friend from work who was a single mother of two small children and never seemed to have the time for anything. I jumped into my car, drove over to her house, walked, in and said, "Put me to work." At first she didn't really believe it, but we ended up having a great time, cleaning like mad, taking time out to feed and play with the kids, and then diving back into the chores.

......................

Charity is the bone shared with the dog when you are just as hungry as the dog.

—*Jack London*

# Flying High

I flew into O'Hare Airport and had a two-hour layover before my connecting flight. So I went to the first bar I could find, ordered a drink, opened my book, and proceeded to wait out the time. Somewhere around the halfway point, I pulled out my ticket to double-check the time of departure and flight number. The gate I was leaving from was almost at the opposite end of the airport, so I left what I though was plenty enough time to get there and check in. By the time I made it all the way over to the right gate I was almost the last person in line to board. That's when I realized my ticket was missing. There I was, checking every pocket, emptying the contents of my briefcase, rechecking my pockets, and all the time I had this sick feeling in my stomach that I had left the ticket on the table in the cocktail lounge at the other end of the airport. Just as I was about to go into a major panic, a man comes running up to the gate and says, "I found this ticket on a chair in the bar. When I saw what flight it was for, I figured maybe I could catch you in time." I barely had time to thank him before I was rushed onto the plane and the doors closed.

........................

The course of human history is determined, not by what happens in the skies, but by what takes place in our hearts.

—*Sir Arthur Keith*

........................

The ideals which have lighted my way, and time after time have given me new courage to face life cheerfully, have been Kindness, Beauty, and Truth. . . . The trite subjects of human efforts—possessions, outward success, luxury— have always seemed to me contemptible.

—*Albert Einstein*

# Take My Seat

I was standing in line getting ready to board a plane when this guy comes rushing up to the ticket counter. He had obviously been running like O. J. Simpson through the terminal and was furious when the woman at the counter told him his reservation had been cleared and his seat given away. She offered to get him a confirmed seat on the next flight, which unfortunately was not leaving for nearly five hours, but he would have none of it. He started screaming about how important it was that he get to Chicago by seven, how irresponsible the airline was when, after all, he had a confirmed ticket, how he wanted to see the supervisor, and on and on and on.

Finally he stopped his tirade and, in a very quite voice, said, "I'm really sorry. I'm just completely stressed out and I can't believe I am going to miss this meeting." Right then an old man, who had been standing in front of me in the boarding line watching this whole thing, stepped up to the counter and said, "Here, take my seat.

I'm retired and I'm in no real hurry to get anywhere." The guy was so happy and so ashamed at the same time it looked like he was going to cry. Then he took the ticket and got on the plane.

........................

Kindness is a language which the dumb can speak,
the deaf can understand.

—*C. N. Bovee*

........................

Man should not consider his material possessions his own,
but common to all, so as to share them without hesitation
when others are in need.

—*St. Thomas Aquinas*

aat
AFP
06.17.10

# Words of Comfort

I grew up in what we would now call a dysfunctional family. My parents materially were quite well off, but we lived amidst emotional chaos and confusion in a wealthy suburb of Philadelphia. As with most children, I simply assumed that this was the way it was and that the problems, the undercurrents of anger and hostility, were somehow my fault. One day when I was still very young, after a particularly painful and confusing series of interactions with my parents, our maid took me aside to talk to me. She told me that she did not care if it cost her her job, she just could not continue to be a silent observer. She told me that my parents were crazy, that they were acting badly, and not at all like good loving parents should act toward their children. She told me that I was a good, sweet girl and that the situation was not my fault. It must have taken a lot of courage for her to do that. Not only to overcome the natural hesitation to intervene between parents and children, but to take the risk that I would not say something about our talk to my parents. I never did talk about it. It was an incredible gift. Her words gave me the explanation I needed, a way to stop blaming everything on myself.

...................

A gift consists not in what is done or given, but in the intention of the giver or doer.

—*Seneca*

...................

Five things constitute perfect virtue: gravity, magnanimity, earnestness, sincerity, and kindness.

—*Confucius*

# The Guardian Angel

One Friday afternoon I was on my way to set up for a book fair in San Francisco. Waiting at a stoplight in front of the convention center, I noticed a handicapped woman on the street corner. She was sitting against a fence, a walker by her side, surrounded by what was probably all of her belongings. As I watched, another woman, perfectly coiffed, in high heels and a power suit, came up to her with a bag. Without a word, the businesswoman proceeded to lay out prepared food, which she had obviously bought "to go," around the street person so that she could easily reach the food from a sitting position. The homeless woman looked on in grateful amazement, as if her guardian angel had appeared out of nowhere just in time. In fact, she had. Three days later, when I was leaving the convention center, I passed the same woman leaning against the same fence. This time, a man in a van was at the stoplight, honking and holding money out to the woman. She was trying to move, but couldn't get up. Quickly, I ran to the van, grabbed the money, and brought it to her. I felt so happy to see people taking care of this woman, and pleased that my weekend was bracketed by tokens of generosity.

......................

Kindness is the noblest weapon to conquer with.

—*American proverb*

......................

There is a Law that man should love his neighbor as himself. In a few hundred years it should be as natural to mankind as breathing or the upright gait; but if he does not learn it he must perish.

—*Alfred Adler*

# Lost and Found

My girlfriend and I are avid backpackers. I can't even describe the feeling I get after we lock up the car and hit the trail, and every step is one step farther into the hills and one step farther away from all the crazy stuff that goes on in the world. In my mind it is such a different reality once we are on the trail, and I guess that is why I always put all my "worldly" things in a small green zip-up bag and stuff it away in a corner of my backpack. I mean everything—my wallet, with all my ID, credit cards, license, etc., all my money, my keys—everything you need to survive in the modern world and everything that is irrelevant back in the woods.

This particular trip was a five-day trek through some of the most beautiful parts of the Cascades. As we headed back down toward the parking area where we had left the car, I was really sad to be leaving what to me was such a simple and beautiful way of living. I could just feel the tension and anxiety beginning to creep back into my body as we got closer and closer to civilization. When we finally got to the car there was a small piece of paper tucked under the windshield-wiper blade that read, "left rear tire." I walked back and looked at the left rear tire but it was fine. The note made no sense to me at all—three seconds back into the world and already lunacy. Then I started fishing through my backpack for my green bag. It wasn't there. I looked back at the left rear tire—there was the bag. I have no idea when I lost it, I have no idea who found it, or how they ever found my car amid all the possible parking places in that part of the Cascades. My keys, my wallet, nearly $100 in cash, all neatly tucked in my zip-up green bag sitting on top of my left rear tire. Thank you, whoever you are, you gave me back much more than you know.

......................

By the accident of fortune a man may rule the world for a time, but by virtue of love and kindness he may rule the world forever.

—*Lao-Tsu*

......................

I feel no need for any other faith than my faith in the
kindness of human beings . . . I am so absorbed in
the wonder of earth and the life upon it that I cannot
think of heaven and angels.

*—Pearl S. Buck*

......................

Kindness makes the difference between passion and
caring. Kindness is tenderness, kindness is love, perhaps
greater than love . . . kindness is goodwill, kindness says
"I want you to be happy." Kindness comes very close to
the benevolence of God.

*—Randolph Ray*

AFP
3/2010

# Sunshine on a Rainy Day

I have been going to the same bagel/coffee shop every Sunday for years. One morning in the middle of a great dreary drizzly weekend, I trudged in dripping wet with my newspaper carefully tucked under my overcoat and ordered my usual bagel with lox and cream cheese and an espresso. I was casually informed that my coffee had already been paid for. I looked around expecting to see some friend sitting somewhere but didn't, and when I asked, the young woman at the register just smiled and said someone paid for twenty coffees and you are number eight. I sat there for almost an hour, reading my paper, and watching more surprised people come in to find their morning coffee pre-paid. There we all were, furtively at first and then with big funny smiles on our faces, looking at everyone else in the restaurant trying to figure out who had done this incredible thing, but mostly just enjoying the experience as a group. It was a beautiful blast of sunshine on an otherwise overcast winter day.

# Practice
# Random Acts of Kindness!

❧ Take the opportunity in conversations with friends to tell them about kindnesses you have experienced and ask about their experiences. Just talking about acts of kindness brings them alive in the world.

❧ Get your children to go through their toys and put aside those they want to donate to children who are less fortunate.

❧ Buy a giant box of candy at the theatre, take one and pass it down the row to share.

❧ Next time you go to the ice-cream parlor, pay for a few free cones to be given to the next kids to come in.

❧ If you have an infirmed person living near you, offer to do the grocery shopping for him or her.

❧ PICK up the mail for a senior or someone else who could use the assistance.

❧ SEND a fax to someone you don't know and start a random acts of kindness chain fax letter.

❧ IF there is a garden you pass frequently and enjoy, stop by one day and leave a note letting the occupants know how much pleasure their garden gives you.

❧ MAKE a dedication on your local radio station to all those people who smiled at strangers today.

# The Winter Coat

A friend of mine was going back east to college. Not only was it her first time away from home but, even more overwhelming to a California baby, it was going to be her first true winter. She spent many months looking for the perfect winter coat, a task all the more difficult when even long pants seemed stifling. Finally, two days before her departure, she found the coat that would keep her from getting frostbite and maybe even homesick. Unfortunately, the store didn't have the size she needed, although one of their other locations thirty miles away did. In desperation, she told the saleswoman her situation, who then proceeded to console her by promising that she would "take care of it." Two days and a few logistical phone calls later, the saleswoman met my friend at the airport gate, perfect-fitting coat in hand. The saleswoman was definitely acting above and beyond the call of duty, since I'm sure her job description didn't require her to deal with airport parking.

........................

The government in which I believe is that which is based on mere moral sanction . . . the real law lives in the kindness of our hearts. If our hearts are empty, no law or political reform can fill them.

—*Leo Tolstoy*

........................

Believe nothing, O monks, merely because you have been told it. . . . Do not believe what your teacher tells you merely out of respect for the teacher. But whatsoever, after due examination and analysis, you find to be kind, conducive to the good, the benefit, the welfare of all beings—that doctrine believe and cling to, and take it as your guide.

—*Buddha*

# The House Fire

We recently had the traumatic experience of having our house burn down, followed by the equally unsettling experience of trying to deal with the insurance company. How do you prove what you lost when it is completely and totally gone?

Our home was built over fifty years ago and, surprisingly, the city still had original blueprints on file. This proved at first to be more of a problem than a help, because we had completely remodeled five years before it burned, adding on an entirely new floor, extending the house out in the backyard, and building a real garage to replace the tiny box common to homes built in the thirties. Needless to say, the insurance company generously offered to replace the house as specified on the original blueprints. We of course had had a drawer full of pictures showing the remodeling job, but that drawer was gone along with everything else. Other than our word and that of friends and neighbors, we had no proof of what we had lost.

Our problem was mentioned in a paragraph in the local newspaper, and a few days later we received a photo album in the mail filled with pictures of our house! A man who had been an architecture student at the time we remodeled our home had done a project on upgrading instead of destroying housing stock and, unbeknownst to us, had used our house as a visual example. He had done a complete photo history: before, during, and after. In his letter, his told us that it had all be quite accidental—that the very day he started looking for a project was the first day our contractor showed up to start working. He had approached him to find out what they were going to do, and our contractor had been very cooperative, showing him all the plans and promising to show him all the gritty details as he progressed. When we showed our insurance adjuster the photos, we could see him gulp—and they ended up paying even more than we had expected.

125

All things whatsoever ye would that men should do to you,
do ye even so to them: for this is the law of the Prophets.

*—Matthew 7:12*

He that is kind is free, though he is a slave; he that is evil
is a slave, though he be a king.

—*St. Augustine*

126

. . . . . . . . . . . . . . . . . . . . .

Compassionate the mountains rise
Dim with the wistful dimness of old eyes
That, having looked on life time out of mind,
Know that the simple gift of being kind
Is greater than all wisdom of the wise.

—*DuBose Heyward*

# On the Bus

I ride the bus to and from work every day—it's about a thirty-five-minute trip. When you commute like I do, you have a real appreciation for the difference between sitting down, which allows you to either doze off or read and just relax, and standing up, during which you are constantly being tossed to one side or another, trying not to smash into other standees and constantly moving out of the way so people can get on or off. It makes you develop a keen sense of strategy for getting a seat. I've discovered that if I cut across the hill a few blocks to catch the bus earlier in its route, it greatly increases my odds of finding a seat. There is one elderly woman who is pretty much on the same schedule as I am and before my discovery I used to get on the bus and she would already be there—usually seated while I remained standing. After my discovery, she would get on the bus and sometimes end up standing while I was already seated. It made me feel a little odd, like I had somehow cheated her, but I did not give up my seat.

One day coming back from work I was standing when I was suddenly hit by this wave of nausea. It felt like I was going to pass out, but I was trying very hard not to make a scene. Suddenly I felt a hand on my arm guiding me down into a seat. It was the woman from my morning bus whom I almost never saw going back. Very gently she helped me into what had been her seat and then hovered over me in a wonderfully protective way to give me some privacy to disappear in. By the time we got back to our neighborhood, I felt well enough to thank her and get home. Ever since that day, I always give her my seat in the morning; in fact, I look forward to it.

......................

What wisdom can you find that is greater than kindness?

—*Jean Jacques Rousseau*

......................

I believe that man will not merely endure; he will prevail.
He is immortal, not because he alone among the creatures
has an inexhaustible voice, but because he has a soul,
a spirit capable of kindness and compassion.

—*William Faulkner*

......................

We may have all come on different ships, but we're in
the same boat now.

—*Martin Luther King, Jr.*

# Automotive Angel

For many years, our next-door neighbor was this very sweet and unusual old woman. Her husband had died quite young and she had lived alone ever since her children grew up and moved out. When my brother and I were young, she always treated us as real people, not just a couple of kids. She would talk to us seriously about what was happening in our lives, and actually took an interest in things like the wins and losses of our baseball teams. She also had what at the time was a really hot car—a silver 1957 Chevy—that she took great care of. As she got older, her son took over the duties of occasionally washing and polishing the car, but then he moved out of state.

One day my brother and I were at our parents' house for Thanksgiving dinner and we noticed that her poor old Chevy was looking very sad. Later that night we snuck into her driveway, washed the car inside and out, waxed it, and polished all the chrome; when we were done it was shining just like a floor model.

That was nearly five years ago, and since then we have made regular guerrilla raids into her driveway. I don't think she knows who is doing it, but my mother reports that she has taken to going "cruising" in her car, and always laughs and tells my mother she has an "automotive angel."

........................

Our brightest blazes of gladness are commonly kindled by unexpected sparks.

—*Dr. Johnson*

........................

I keep my ideals, because in spite of everything I still believe that people are really good at heart.

—*Anne Frank*

# Forgiveness

Several months ago, I found myself driving in Los Angeles through morning rush hour traffic. Traffic was heavy, but everyone was going quite fast. Suddenly a white Mazda RX7 in the slow lane spun out, doing four complete circles across the freeway. I stared in disbelief as cars swerved to avoid the whirling white dervish. By some miracle, all the traffic missed the car, which came to rest on the opposite side of the freeway, in the fast lane, facing the wrong way. No one stopped; everyone continued on as though nothing had happened.

I pulled off the freeway, got out of my car, walked to the Mazda, opened the door, and pulled out a sobbing, semihysterical woman who kept saying, "Did you see what they did? They ran me off the road." I put my arms around the woman, who collapsed into them and sobbed as though her heart would break. She finally calmed down enough to explain that a blue Bronco had forced her off the road, causing her car to spin out. There we stood—two women, total strangers, holding and comforting one another on a busy freeway. Suddenly a third car, a blue Bronco, stopped. A third woman jumped out, also crying. She ran over to the woman in my arms, saying over and over again, "I am so sorry; I didn't see you; please forgive me." The first woman turned from me to the newcomer, and they melted into a sobbing embrace of "please forgive me's" and "it's OK's." When both women had calmed down, we figured out how to get the Mazda turned in the right direction, and, once accomplished, jumped back in our own cars and went on our way.

....................

When I give I give myself.

—*Walt Whitman*

....................

T'was her thinking of others that made you think of her.

—*Elizabeth Browning*

# Thoughts on
# Random Acts of Kindness

I don't like this *random* word. I can understand the re-framing of the notion of random violence, but for me, even random kindness triggers a similar shrug of my shoulders, a feeling of powerlessness. I hate the word. I've taken to calling it the *r-word.*

I'm not interested in ideas that seem to encourage the notion of being a passive agent. And while I ac-knowledge that sometimes life is painful and difficult, I also don't subscribe to "shit happens." *Random* is the kind of adjective that goes with a verb like *happens*—no actor, only the acted upon.

For a few years now I've been learning to bring more consciousness to my living, to pay attention to patterns, to use the ones that support me in new ways, to change the ones that don't. It's helping me to live more deeply, to find the intention beneath my intention.

My exploration has included reading such physicists as David Bohm. He is helping me to see how the uni-verse is a living organism with an intricate pattern.

When the universe makes sense to us, he calls those patterns the unfolded or explicate order. Those aspects that we have yet to name or unravel, or even fathom, he calls enfolded. It reminds me of encoded, and it feels to me like "random" events occur as a part of these still-enfolded patterns. Psychologist Stan Grof wrote in his book *The Holotropic Mind* that believing in a random universe is like thinking that a tornado could blow through a junkyard and assemble a 747 from the parts it found there. I liked that when I read it; it gave me a kind of "so there" feeling about the r-word.

But this isn't an intellectual argument for me, and name-dropping two brilliant people hasn't done anything to reduce the powerful visceral feelings I have about this word. That's because at bottom I believe that the universe is alive and mysterious, ultimately benevolent and orderly.

So I wrestle with "random" kindness, and try to imagine that it means those blessings that seem to appear around me without any effort on my part. Then I feel grateful for being able to take in the beauty or the love that surrounds me. That feels like a grace—my ability to really take in a kindness is as miraculous as the kindness itself. And I don't believe it's random.

I know that I have been the fortunate indirect object of much generosity—songs, sculptures, great and funny stories. I know they were not created with me in mind. But they were created or discovered, and then shared with intention.

I love intention, and consciousness, and discovery, and synchronicity. I am in awe of the creative mind at play in the creative universe. I believe in the magic of the unconscious mind, and when mine sends a message to my awareness, that's the universe revealing itself to me, that's God and me dancing. That's joy and mystery. That's not random.

Random acts of kindness. It has such a beautiful ring to it. A part of the beauty is undoubtedly the turnaround from that ugliest and most frightening of all phrases: random acts of violence. We all know of, or at least we know the deep personal fear of, random acts of violence. Haven't we all considered at some point that anytime, from anywhere, it could come, and for no apparent reason we—or someone we love—could be struck down? It's so easy to fear. It's so easy to create an almost palpable reality out of our imagined terror. Random acts of kindness ring pure and true as an antidote to that fear, as life-confirming revolutionary acts.

The word *kind* itself offers us so much insight: the *Oxford English Dictionary* begins its unraveling of the word *kind* by defining it as "the place or property, the character or quality derived from birth or native constitution. We are of that 'kind'—to act according to one's nature; to do what is natural to one; by nature, naturally, the natural state, form or condition; the manner or way natural or proper to anyone."

Is not one of the great gifts of any act of kindness that it "brings us back," that it makes us feel that we have somehow returned to a place, to a feeling, that is somehow permanent, deeply rooted, and unchanging even as we begin once again to drift away? Kindness is at the heart of our belief that people are basically good. Kindness is the vehicle for all our hope that in the larger struggle between good and evil, good will prevail because ultimately we will return to kindness. It is our natural condition, our instinctual impulse to extend a hand.

And every hand we extend, every act of kindness we commit, sends a ripple out into the world that is magnified by every life it encounters. Fear and its real-world manifestation—violence—is stark and dramatic. It can temporarily consume, take over, and crowd out everything else.

Kindness is soft and subtle. It permeates everything it comes in contact with, remains as a permanent reminder of what could and should be.

What about acts of kindness toward ourselves? OK, so they're not random, but for a lot of people they are probably more difficult to do, much harder to remember, and maybe even more important in the long run. A friend of mine calls doing such things the new frontier. I like to think of them as refilling the cup. Kindness cannot flow from an empty cup, and the complex web of interactions we all seem to be caught up in these days almost demands that we empty everything we have and then some on a constant basis. So it is crucial that we re-fuel our own spirits so that we will want to be compassionate to others.

It's not an easy thing to do. Our jobs demand our time and energy because that part of us is bought and paid for. Then for many of us, our jobs ask even more—that we take them home, worry about them, and use up our precious resources of time, energy, and focus, all the while putting our own needs, our own desires, the things we want to do, farther and farther on the back burner.

Then comes the family. Kids, spouses, parents, siblings all make demands on us, both specific and general. Please pick up the pictures, drop off the dry cleaning, take me to soccer practice, call the insurance guy for me, check on this or that, do the grocery shopping, make sure the laundry is done, buy me some new socks . . . the list never ends. And for many people, particularly those sweet, loving, generous souls who usually end up carrying such a list, the doing for others not only never stops, but actually escalates as the "others" get more and more used to it and take it more and more for granted.

So what starts out as generous acts of kindness can gradually become hollow acts of servitude. The giver is doubly impoverished, because the acts themselves are no longer gifts but rather expected routines and because the burden of the obligations precludes the possibility of giving to oneself. In this way, those nonrandom acts of kindness toward friends, family, and lovers—the ones we all tend to assume come so easily and flow so freely—can actually prove to be not only the most difficult to maintain in the pure spirit of kindness, but can in fact turn so easily into vehicles of barter and bonds of obligation.

Think hard about all the people in your life, about times when you received some gift of generosity from them that penetrated your heart and resonated with a clear, pure feeling of kindness. When was the last time one of your acts of kindness toward someone within your circle was clearly received in that way? If we are truthful, for most of us the answer is that it occurs all too infrequently, and the saddest part is that for all we do for each other, we have managed to reduce it from the magical realm of gifts freely and generously given to that of barter and obligation—currency and duties tallied up and traded back and forth.

No doubt there are many reasons why we fall into this sad pattern. But I believe that at the root of the problem is the saddest fact of all—that we take such poor care of our own needs and desires, that we all end up in a constant state of not having enough, not getting what we need, and wanting, always wanting, and expecting someone else to provide it.

For random acts of kindness to flourish we need to begin in the hardest of all places, our own hearts. To reap a bountiful harvest of random acts of kindness, we need to begin by simple acts of kindness toward ourselves. Then we can truly give from overflow, from a heart brimming with loving kindness.

# Acknowledgments

We would like to extend our boundless gratitude to those who shared their stories and suggestions:

Dawna Markova, Daphne Rose Kingma, Karen Bouris, Julie Bennett, Mary Jane Ryan, Will Glennon, Molli Nickell, Arthur Naiman, Tom Modic, Shirley Davalos, Tobias Stead, Pat Adler, Katherine Falk, Aaron Burack, Beth Nitzbey, Lewis Rambo, Robyn Brode, Martha Jackson, Nancy Evans, David Mack, Gail Derrin, Carol Brown, Bahman Sheikh-Ol-Eslami, Charlotte Burchard, Beverly Potter, Sebastian Orfali, Marilyn Chandler, John McEntyre, Donald McIlraith, Vanessa Carlisle, Roy Carlisle, Joan Edwards, Joel Drucker, Jane Goodwin, Ed Blonz, Marty Jacobs, Gary Rosenberg, Peris Gumz, Anne Powell, Dale LaPointe, Sheila Downes, Irene Imfeld, Tory Lee, Barbara Alexander, Adrienne Candy, Matthew and Ellen Cohen, Jerry Cimmet, Karen Shannon, Jane Seitel, Eric Mellencamp, Frances Wong, Damian Glennon, Alice Marie Alexander, Chris Sechley, Susanna Bluestein,

Patricia Munson, Dina Huniu, Paula Gotch, Steve Worrell, Tami Cosgrove, Johnathan Peltham, Robert Bastian, Jane Dickson, Phu Nguyen, Peggy McQueen, and Molly Fumia.

# Join the Kindness Movement

The Kindness Movement is an international movement dedicated to making the world a kinder place. Our goal is to demonstrate the extraordinary power and importance of simple human kindness by promoting the practice of kind acts, large and small, on a regular basis. People everywhere are discovering that when kindness is expressed, healthy relationships are created, community connections are nourished, and people are inspired to pass kindness on to others.

The Random Acts of Kindness™ Foundation supports the Kindness Movement by providing leadership, inspiration, guidance, educational and promotional materials, and opportunities to connect with people around the world. Through the dissemination of ideas and the development of materials and programs, we help our coordinators incorporate kindness into thousands of communities and schools.

More than 30,000 people in the United States coordinate kindness projects in their local communities, and more than 800,000 students are engaged in Random Acts of Kindness projects.

RANDOM ACTS OF KINDNESS WEEK
is celebrated annually in February during the week of Valentine's Day.

WORLD KINDNESS WEEK
is celebrated annually in November during the week of World Kindness Day, November 13.

For more information on getting involved,
please contact us:

> THE RANDOM ACTS OF KINDNESS FOUNDATION
> 1727 Tremont Place
> Denver, CO 80202
> 1-800-660-2811
> *www.actsofkindness.org*
> e-mail: rakinfo@actsofkindness.org

# Send Us Your Random Acts of Kindness

If the stories in this book inspired you, then help spread the flow of kindness back into the world. Send us your stories or suggestions for how we can all put a little more kindness into our daily lives. Don't worry about making them perfect, just tell them in your own words. If writing is difficult for you, tell them into a tape recorder and send us the tape. Send to:

Conari Press
An imprint of Red Wheel/Weiser, LLC
500 Third Street, Suite 230
San Francisco, CA 94107

# To Our Readers

Conari Press, an imprint of Red Wheel/Weiser, publishes books on topics ranging from spirituality, personal growth, and relationships to women's issues, parenting, and social issues. Our mission is to publish quality books that will make a difference in people's lives—how we feel about ourselves and how we relate to one another. We value integrity, compassion, and receptivity, both in the books we publish and in the way we do business.

Our readers are our most important resource, and we value your input, suggestions, and ideas about what you would like to see published. Please feel free to contact us, to request our latest book catalog, or to be added to our mailing list.

Conari Press
An imprint of Red Wheel/Weiser, LLC
500 Third Street, Suite 230
San Francisco, CA 94107
*www.redwheelweiser.com*